ROUTLEDGE LIBRARY EDITIONS:
ADULT EDUCATION

Volume 18

ADULT EDUCATION AND THE CHALLENGES OF THE 1990S

ADULT EDUCATION AND THE CHALLENGES OF THE 1990S

Edited by
WALTER LEIRMAN AND JINDRA KULICH

LONDON AND NEW YORK

First published in 1987 by Croom Helm Ltd

This edition first published in 2019
by Routledge
2 Park Square, Milton Park, Abingdon, Oxon OX14 4RN

and by Routledge
52 Vanderbilt Avenue, New York, NY 10017

Routledge is an imprint of the Taylor & Francis Group, an informa business

© 1987 Walter Leirman and Jindra Kulich

All rights reserved. No part of this book may be reprinted or reproduced or utilised in any form or by any electronic, mechanical, or other means, now known or hereafter invented, including photocopying and recording, or in any information storage or retrieval system, without permission in writing from the publishers.

Trademark notice: Product or corporate names may be trademarks or registered trademarks, and are used only for identification and explanation without intent to infringe.

British Library Cataloguing in Publication Data
A catalogue record for this book is available from the British Library

ISBN: 978-1-138-32224-0 (Set)
ISBN: 978-0-429-43000-8 (Set) (ebk)
ISBN: 978-1-138-36615-2 (Volume 18) (hbk)
ISBN: 978-1-138-36667-1 (Volume 18) (pbk)
ISBN: 978-0-429-43037-4 (Volume 18) (ebk)

Publisher's Note
The publisher has gone to great lengths to ensure the quality of this reprint but points out that some imperfections in the original copies may be apparent.

Disclaimer
The publisher has made every effort to trace copyright holders and would welcome correspondence from those they have been unable to trace.

ADULT EDUCATION AND THE CHALLENGES OF THE 1990s

Edited by
WALTER LEIRMAN and JINDRA KULICH

CROOM HELM
London • New York • Sydney

© 1987 Walter Leirman and Jindra Kulich
Croom Helm Ltd, Provident House, Burrell Row,
Beckenham, Kent, BR3 1AT

Croom Helm Australia, 44-50 Waterloo Road,
North Ryde, 2113, New South Wales

Published in the USA by
Croom Helm
in association with Methuen, Inc.
29 West 35th Street
New York, NY 10001

British Library Cataloguing in Publication Data

Adult education and the challenge of the
  1990's. — (Croom Helm series in
  international adult education).
  1. Adult education
  I. Leirman, Walter II. Kulich, Jindra
  374   LC5215
  ISBN 0-7099-4169-2

Library of Congress Cataloging-in-Publication Data

ISBN 0-7099-4169-2

Printed and bound in Great Britain
by Billing & Sons Limited, Worcester.

CONTENTS

Preface

1. ADULT EDUCATION : MOVEMENT AND DISCIPLINE
   BETWEEN THE GOLDEN SIXTIES AND THE IRON
   EIGHTIES
   Walter Leirman 1

2. PRODUCTIVITY AND TIME : A REFLECTION
   ABOUT THE FUTURE
   Tamas Palasthy 29

3. EDUCATION, PRODUCTION, DEVELOPMENT AND
   TECHNOLOGICAL INNOVATION
   Ettore Gelpi 41

4. PERSPECTIVE OF AN ENVIRONMENTAL ORIENTED
   ECONOMY
   Theo Potma 56

5. ECOLOGICAL EDUCATION A FAILING PRACTICE ?
   OR : IS THE ECOLOGICAL MOVEMENT AN EDUCA-
   TIONAL MOVEMENT ?
   Marianne Gronemeyer 70

6. PEACEMAKING IN THE COMMUNITY, THE NATION,
   AND THE WORLD
   Paul Wehr 84

7. PEACE EDUCATION : LEARNING HOW TO TRANS-
   FORM A LIFE-WORLD THREATENED BY VIOLENCE
   Walter Leirman 98

8. MULTICULTURAL SOCIETIES IN NORTH-WESTERN EUROPE
   Eugeen Roosens 118

9. MULTICULTURAL EDUCATION AS A TASK OF ADULT EDUCATION : OBSERVATIONS FROM CANADA AND THE FEDERAL REPUBLIC OF GERMANY
   Joachim Knoll 134

10. THE MORAL BASE OF DEVELOPMENT
    Louis Baeck 148

11. DIALOGUE TOWARDS DEVELOPMENT AND THE DEVELOPMENT OF DIALOGUE
    Antonio Faundez 159

12. THE UNIVERSITY AND ADULT EDUCATION : THE NEWEST ROLE AND RESPONSIBILITY OF THE UNIVERSITY
    Jindra Kulich 170

13. TRAINING SYSTEMS FOR FUTURE ADULT EDUCATORS
    Borivoj Samolovčev 191

14. ADULT EDUCATION AND THE COMPUTER
    Thomas Keenan 205

PREFACE

The fourteen papers contained in this volume were commissioned for the international conference "Adult Education and the Challenges of the 1990s : Peace, Development, Employment, Environment, Technology", held at the Catholic University of Leuven, Belgium, September 28 to October 1, 1986. Some 220 participants from 22 countries took part in the conference. The papers were presented in English, French, German or Netherlandic (Dutch), with simultaneous translation into Dutch, English, French, and German.
The conference dealt with six major existential issues of the final decades of our century : Labour and Employment Education, Environment and Ecological Education, Peacemaking and Peace Education, Intercultural Relations and Multicultural Education, Development between North and South, and University and Adult Education. Papers on these issues were presented against the background of the introductory paper which set the framework. The final paper dealt with Adult Education and the Computer.
The introductory paper by Walter Leirman, "Adult Education : Movement and Discipline between the Golden Sixties and the Iron Eighties" contains a retrospective analysis of the development of theory and practice of adult education between the educationally optimistic early sixties and the crisis-laden eighties, combined with a succinct analysis and reflection on major issues of our times : employment, environment, peace, intercultural relations, Third World development and technology; the paper closes with a proposed new socio-communicative paradigm for an ecological man-world and education.

Preface

Tamas Palasthy's paper, "Productivity and Time : A reflection about the Future", outlines the basic economic interdependence of all the regions in the world, attempts to clarify the most important factors which determine these interdependencies in order to situate the West in a worldwide context, and presents solutions to the present economic crisis as depending essentially on a fundamental political choice concerning the future organization of society as the only adjustable internal factor in the West.

Ettore Gelpi in "Education, Production, Development and Technological Innovation" provides an insightful analysis of the disorder in productive and social relationships, the current educational inertia and revitalization of education, transfers of technology and transfers of training, the necessary unity of production, education, cultural adventure and scientific research, the causes of resistance to innovation, and education for innovation.

Theo Potma's paper, "Perspective of an Environmental Oriented Economy", provides an analysis of the relationship between environment and welfare of society, and between environment and the economy, proposing the need for a realistic approach of the 'hard-ware' possibilities on our globe and the 'soft-ware' possibilities to change our social behaviour; the paper also presents a case study of a successful intervention in a national discussion on energy policy in the Netherlands.

Marianne Gronemeyer in "Ecological Education a Failing Practice ? OR : Is the Ecological Movement an Educational Movement ?" puts forward an interesting thesis that the ecological education and ecological movement are both failures because they have been blurred and exchanged their objectives, with ecological movements now engaging in ecological learning while ecological education now is aiming at persuasion; the author asks for the acts of sharing, doubting, considering and inquiry in our quest for ecological education.

Paul Wehr's paper, "Peacemaking in the Community, the Nation, and the World", proposes that a central problem of our time is the absence of peace and security at all these levels and provides suggestions for ways and means of formal and informal education to assist in solving this problem, and outlines assumptions about peacemaking, dimensions of building a national peacemaking capacity, and institutions for peacemaking.

Walter Leirman in "Peace Education : Learning how to Transform a Life-World Threatened by Violence" defines various concepts of 'peace', classifies types of peacemaking and peace education, analyses the peace movement as part of the 'new social movements', and stresses that peace education as a form of critical pedagogy must combine reflection and action, but cannot replace the latter.

Eugeen Roosens' paper, "Multicultural Societies in North-Western Europe", provides an analysis of the situation and problems of the (migrant) cultural/ethnic minorities in the last two decades and looks into the attempts and failures at dealing with the integration or assimilation of these groups; the paper also offers suggestions for accomplishing a multicultural society in the specific conditions of North-Western Europe.

Joachim Knoll in "Multicultural Education as a Task of Adult Education : Observations from Canada and the Federal Republic of Germany" deals first with the conceptual and theoretical analysis and then moves on to consideration of the tasks and desirabilities of multicultural education illustrated by case studies of Canada and the Federal Republic of Germany; the paper closes with a statement of multicultural education as an essential part of a necessary new behaviour in the future.

Louis Baeck's paper, "The Moral Base of Development", provides an overview of major developments since 1945 in East-West conflict and North-South tension, an analysis of the crisis of development theories from "mainstream thinking" to the "dependencia school". The author then exposes a moral base for development, exemplified by the Latin-American basista movement (Movimientos de Base).

Antonio Faundez in "Dialogue Towards Development and the Development of Dialogue" engages in a philosophical treatise leading to a statement "To consider development as a process of education also means that education should be considered as a dialogical process of development, as they are inseparable. This is the reason why education for development also implies the development of education. But such a conception supposes a different interpretation of the two concepts."

Preface

Jindra Kulich's paper, "The University and Adult Education : The Newest Role and Responsibility of the University" outlines the place of the university in lifelong learning and education, traces the historical development and current provision of part-time degree credit programs, general non-credit continuing education, professional continuing education and community service by the universities, and provides the rationale for such an involvement.

Borivoj Samolovcev in "Training Systems for Future Adult Educators" traces the development of non-credit and credit training programs, provides many examples of current training provision in a number of countries as well as of in-service training, and pleads for turning away from pragmatic-technological orientation of training to the pedagogy of essence, to humanistic orientation; the paper also deals with an overview of research in adult education.

In the final paper by Thomas Keenan, "Adult Education and the Computer", questions and issues such as computers and learning styles, computers for computation, computers as tools for communication, computer assisted learning, computer simulation and gaming, computers as scholars' work stations, and computers as windows on tomorrow, are dealt with.

Those papers which were originally not written in English have been translated for this publication. In translation, every attempt has been made to maintain the personal flavour of the original, if necessary at the expense of standard English usage, while clarity of the presentation was of paramount consideration. The editors decided against imposing uniformity of spelling usage and opted instead for staying with the English or American spelling as it was used by the writers or translators.

The publication of the fourteen papers is intended to make the consideration of these important issues of our time available to a broader international audience beyond those who were able to attend the conference. Together with the present book, a 80' videotape has been produced by the Audiovisual Department of the K.U. Leuven, containing interviews and discussions with most of the authors and some conference participants. This complement can be ordered from the organizing Afdeling Sociale Pedagogiek, K.U. Leuven, Vesaliusstraat 2, B-3000 LEUVEN - Belgium.

Preface

In the view of the editors, as well as of the Series Editor, the approach taken in the organization of the conference and the papers is unique in its combination of the points of departure informing the analysis of the situation and the challenges facing adult educators.

Walter Leirman
Jindra Kulich

Chapter One
ADULT EDUCATION : MOVEMENT AND DISCIPLINE BETWEEN
THE GOLDEN SIXTIES AND THE IRON EIGHTIES

Walter LEIRMAN
Cath. University of Leuven
Belgium

The future of adult education as a field and as a discipline cannot be separated from its (recent) past. Past experience if well evaluated, constitutes a cornerstone of future action.
   The present introduction will therefore take on the form of a <u>retrospective tale</u> of significant developments experienced within our own unit and the discipline at large, combined with a <u>systematic yet succinct analysis and reflection</u> on major issues of our times : <u>employment</u>, <u>environment</u>, <u>peace</u>, <u>intercultural relations</u>, <u>third world development</u> and <u>technology</u>.

<u>Starting in a climate of existential and educational optimism</u>
To us, 1966 was a golden year in a golden decade. The concept of a new section of "social pedagogy" was worked out in relation to an international congress on "the cultural functionary", organized by the "Studiegroep voor Cultuurbevordering" (Study Group for Cultural Advancement) in 1964 in Brussels. It was presented by Prof. Cyril De Keyser, who also attracted the later staff group : Prof. J. Stalpers, Prof. J. Vollebergh and the present author.
   Like many other starters of new training and research programs, we not only looked upon ourselves as pioneers of a new field of study, but also as innovators of both contents and methods of higher education itself. We would bring the dynamic spirit of youthwork and adult education to the university, and give a better theoretical and professional foundation to the field we all came from. The basic philosophy behind our effort was a mosaic-like mixture of French "éducation permanente", German "Andragogik" and Anglo-Saxon adult education and "planned

change" theory. The first element - éducation permanente or lifelong learning - was brought to us by the writings of B. Cacérès (CACERES, 1964), B. Schwartz (SCHWARTZ, 1977) and R. Lengrand (LENGRAND, 1966), and officialized on the world forum by the 1960 UNESCO-Conference in Montreal. It basically contained three messages : rapid societal changes provoke continually new learning needs in adults; all citizens, and especially those who are socially or culturally deprived, should be given organized educational opportunities to meet their needs; authorities should create a flexible yet fully integrated educational system for all ages and all social groups. The current of "Andragogik", represented by authors like F. Pöggeler (PÖGGELER, 1957) and Th. Ballauf (BALLAUF, 1958) professed similar views, but stressed the need of differentiation between descriptive analysis of institutions, programs and participants on the one hand, and normative reflection and evaluation on the other hand. One of the dominant "Leitbilder" (= guiding images) of the German adult education movement was that of "Mündigkeit" (= emancipated man), which ideally meant the integration of autonomy and social responsibility to be developed in each phase of adult life. However interesting these currents seemed to be, they did not have the character of full-fledged theories based on (empirical) research. It was because of this that the Anglo-Saxon theories of "the dynamics of planned social change" attracted so much of our attention. Here, adult education became part of a world-wide social change enterprise, where "change agents" would guide their "clients" through a process that started with a diagnosis and the establishment of a change relationship, moved towards the setting of goals and the construction and execution of a program, and ended in evaluation, generalization and the termination of the change relationship.

This perspective, developed by K. Lewin, and further elaborated by R. Lippit et al., received its almost universal recognition when W. Bennis, K. Benne and R. Chin published their handbook The Planning of Change for the first time in 1961. The change perspective was now broadened into three global strategies, and applied to many different fields of social practice.

Even though Bennis et al. did not intend it in this way, the "change agent-client system" paradigm was well expressed in the parable of the grasshopper and the owl, presented in the introduction. The story runs like this (BENNIS et al., 1961, p. 3) :

> There is an old parable that has made the rounds about the grasshopper who decided to consult the hoary consultant of the animal kingdom, the owl, about a personal problem. The problem concerned the fact that the grasshopper suffered each winter from severe pains due to the savage temperature. After a number of these painful winters, in which all of the grasshopper's known remedies were of no avail, he presented his case to the venerable and wise owl. The owl, after patiently listening to the grasshopper's misery, so the story goes, prescribed a simple solution. "Simply turn yourself into a cricket and hibernate during the winter". The grasshopper jumped joyously away, profusely thanking the owl for his wise advice. Later however, after discovering that this important knowledge could not be transformed into action, the grasshopper returned to the owl and asked him how he could perform this metamorphosis. The owl replied rather curtly, "Look, I gave you the principle. It's up to you to work out the details !"

Bennis et al. then explained the moral of the story as follows : "How can the man of knowledge utilize his hard won knowledge to help clients and lay personnel ? And conversely, how can the lay public provide information and insight that will aid the man of knowledge, the expert, in his role as helper as well as theory builder ?" (BENNIS et al., 1961, p.3). Within the "new field of change study", adult education was, however, only a small part and it still had to earn its credentials as a scientific discipline - certainly in Europe. In North America, theory building started earlier, due to the efforts of pioneers like C. Houle and C. Verner who came to our university in 1969 to work with us. In our own, Dutch-speaking area of the Netherlands and the Flemish part of Belgium, one author set himself especially to the task of delineating the conceptual framework for a new discipline, which was first called social pedagogy and agology, and finally "andragology" : T. Ten Have (TEN HAVE, 1973). He set out

Adult Education

Figure 1.1

The parable of the owl and the grasshopper : "I gave you the general principle..."

to define a number of essential concepts like "culture", "socio-cultural work", "vorming" (= general education of the whole person), "welzijn" (= well-being) and had a clear influence upon the coining of the term "vormings- en ontwikkelingswerk" (= adult education) to be understood as follows : "Adult education is a process in the person by which he or she arrives at a better understanding of oneself and the actual situation, at a critical evaluation of both and at a conscious and direct handling of the possibilities offered by the societal situation". He also developed a general process theory of adult education, and claimed the status of suprastructural science for such "change" sciences as politilogy and andragology, indicating that they both drew upon basic "mother" sciences like philosophy, psychology and sociology, yet were developing their own theories and models. The concept of andragogy was also put forward as a necessary complement to that of pedagogy, which was the study of the education of children, as opposed to that of the education of adults who were said to have a rich life experience and a clear social responsibility. Although similar developments have taken place elsewhere, there has been no country in the world (with the exception, perhaps, of Yugoslavia) where the construct of andrago(lo)gy has been worked out with so great a consequence, as in the Netherlands, where we witnessed the establishment of several (sub)faculties of "andragogy". This, of course, stirred quite some debate in the early seventies, but that debate quietened by the end of the decade, as it became clear that the global, almost utopian concept had not been buttressed up by substantive research and theory building. I was rather amazed, however, to find out that a similar "andragogy"-debate has started in recent years in North America, following M. Knowles' publication with the same title (KNOWLES, 1970). I was still more amazed to find that Ten Have's work was indirectly drawn into the debate, via an article of two South African scholars, who read and wrote both Dutch and English!

The development of global change models and general frameworks like those of Bennis et al. (BENNIS et al., 1961) or of Ten Have (TEN HAVE, 1973) was in part made possible by the socio-cultural and educational optimism of the mid-sixties that characterized at least the Western and Northern Hemispheres. The "Global Village" was believed to be in a firm orbit of continuous growth and expansion, and science, technology and the U.N. would solve the undeniable but curable problems of the world. This was proved by statistical analyses of the GNP, and by studies where more qualitative aspects were quantified, as is shown in the following diagram used in one of our courses :

Figure 1.2

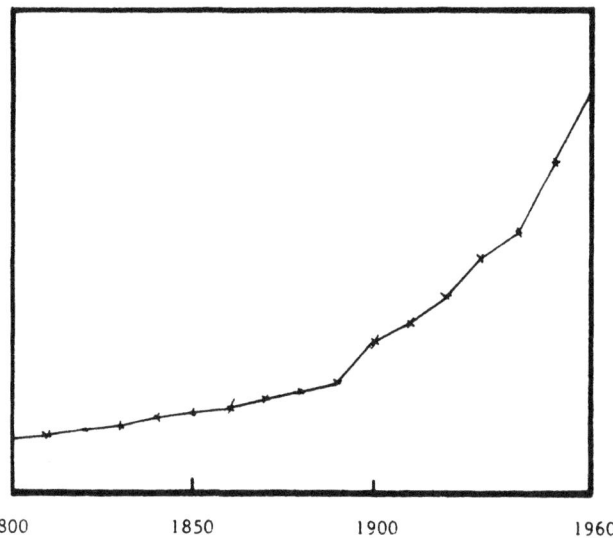

Societal evolution between 1800 and 1960, measured by a combination of 4 variables : increase in knowledge, decreace in deathrate, increase in income and increase in the use of communication (Van Duyne, 1964).

What we are presented with here, is an exponential curve, showing that the evolution between 1900 and 1960 has been about three times "stronger" than the evolution in the whole 19th century. At that time, we only questioned the way in which the variables had been quantified and combined, but not the underlying criteria of selection and the "positive" conclusions drawn from the analysis. With a prospective increase in population, welfare and communication opportunities, there could be no doubt that "permanent education" had nothing but a glorious future in front of it.

The political and economic shockwaves of the late sixties and the early seventies

The so-called youth revolt of May 1968 in Europe, announcing "the long march through the capitalist institutions" provided a first serious disturbance to the welfare optimism of the sixties. Democratization and participation became the new watch-words. However, new "revolutionary" movements sometimes provide the impetus to solve old disputes or to help older emancipatory movements to realize their goals. This was also the case at our own university : the sociolinguistic conflict between the Flemish and the French-speaking communities of Belgium also materialized in this Flemish city, where a leading group of French-speaking professors claimed a bi-lingual status and wanted to realize a "corridor" from Brussels to Leuven/Louvain. Thereupon the whole Flemish community reacted with the demand that the existing Université Catholique de Louvain leave Flemish territory. The national government fell over the issue, and in the end the decision was taken to move the French-speaking university to Ottignies, where the campus of Louvainla-Neuve was erected. To foreigners, what happened in Leuven is difficult to understand, except from a comparison with analogous examples of ethnico-political conflict, like the one between French- and English-speaking Canadians. Although the conflict never took on Northern Irish, South African or Lebanese dimensions, the two universities each developed relations with many foreign institutions and have virtually lived in mutual isolation until the present day. The intercultural conflict has for a long time been an inspiring theme of adult education on both sides of the language border, and there also was a clear link between the Flemish emancipation movement and adult education, but efforts of intercultural, cooperative education in Belgium have been rare exceptions. It is only in recent years that contacts between research centers and adult education institutions on both sides of the language border have been established.

The politico-cultural shock of 1968 also had a more specific impact upon our field and discipline. Closest to us, it activated student protest and participation, in our own programme, and led to curriculum reform.

On a more general level, the field witnessed the rise and expansion of so-called "alternative education", which took its inspiration in the writings and the projects of I. Illich, P. Freire,

Adult Education

O. Negt, S. Neill, the Frankfurt School, etc. The professed goal was no less than to "change society in the direction of a basic democracy through education, combined with political action".

This alternative movement - which was by no means restricted to the field of education - posed a real threat to the "traditional" organizations and institutions which were decried as being bourgeois-conservative and, in some cases, even labelled as dead or decomposing. The dialectic confrontation of "alternative" and "traditional" has, at least in our country, by and large been beneficial : new "forgotten" groups and themes were addressed, and several traditional organizations engaged in serious soul-searching and started renovating their contents, strategies and methods.

At the level of the discipline, a concomitant change of focus took place : from personal to societal education, and from an "adaptive" to an "innovative" perspective. Two currents of pedagogical thinking became very prominent now : on the one hand, German "emancipatory pedagogy" presented by authors like Kl. Mollenhauer (MOLLENHAUER, 1970) and H. Giesecke (GIESECKE, 1973) and basically inspired by the Frankfurt School (especially J. Habermas (HABERMAS, 1970) of the "third" generation), and on the other hand the "conscientization pedagogy" of the Brazilian educator and pedagogue P. Freire (FREIRE, 1970). Leuven became also personally acquainted with Freire when he became doctor honoris causa of our university in 1975.

Being confronted with these related changes in the student movement, in the educational field and in the discipline, we were impelled to give serious thought to our own theoretical position. We became engaged in research projects where the theme of "emancipation" of working-class women, the young generation and inhabitants of deprived neighbourhoods or regions became the central focus of both analysis and educative action. We thus gradually developed a concept of emancipatory science based upon the combination of truth, wellbeing and practicality, and opting for an educational research cycle where reflection and action would dialectically be linked.

From what we have said thus far, it would seem that the switch towards a more critical and socially engaged field and discipline was provoked by new movements and by creative thinkers. What could have been, however, the "objective basis" of such a shift ? At least part of that objective basis became clear in the memorable year of 1972 when the Club of Rome published its first report with the significant title The Limits to Growth (MEADOWS et al., 1977), and when the Opec cartel provoked a first worldwide oil crisis. Based on a study of long-term interaction of five important processes : economic development, population growth, pollution generation, resource depletion and food production, D. Meadows (MEADOWS et al., 1977) and his team made a computer simulation model of the world's evolution from the year 1950 up to the year 2100. They came to the conclusion that if the present patterns of rapid population and capital growth are allowed to continue, the world faces a "disastrous collapse", towards the end of the 21st century. The report drew worldwide attention, and was also greeted with fierce criticism. The Club of Rome took serious notice of these criticisms, and published a second report where 70 variables were accounted for, and regional variations were incorporated. The conclusions were less pessimistic but remained, on the whole, unchanged. In an article, published in 1977, D. Meadows (MEADOWS et al., 1977), presents the following graph of retrospective and prospective world evolution (Figure 1.3).

Meadow's figure (p.10) can only very partially be compared with Figure 1.2 presented earlier, yet it becomes immediately clear that they predict a quite contrary evolution. The Club of Rome authors reached five basic conclusions :

1. There are many factors which will prevent our global society from sustaining its current rates of population and economic growth for many more decades.
2. Our society's most probable mode of accommodation to finite limits is through overshoot and collapse.
3. The delays inherent in our social and ecological systems virtually ensure collapse if we continue to seek change only in response to crises which have already been realized.
4. Policies enacted now are already determining the timing and mode of the shift from exponential growth to global equilibrium.
5. A new and desirable phase of social development is possible, which would leave man in a visible and sustainable balance with his finite environment.

Adult Education

The figure shown here does not contain the pollution and industrial production variables - as does the overall model representation - yet this picture is easier to understand and the general trend remains the same.

Figure 1.3

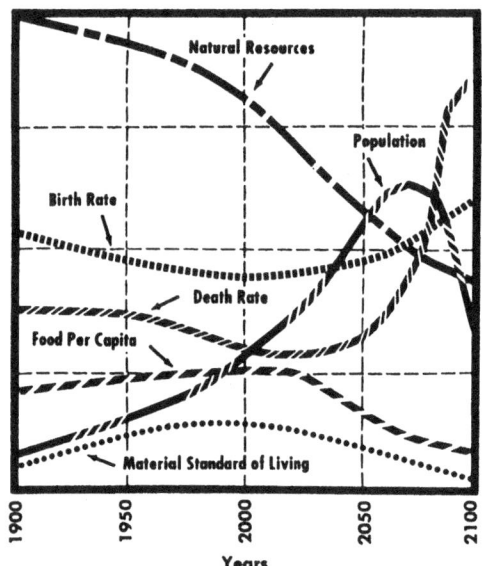

This sample simulation of the global model used by the M.I.T. researchers shows how the depletion of natural resources could halt population growth. This projection, which may be compared with the earlier projection on the front cover, shows a rapidly rising death rate in the latter half of the 21st century.

Global world evolution between 1900 and 2100, based on the long-term interaction of four processes : standard of living, population, food per capita, natural resources, (population is also split into components death rate and birth rate) (Meadows, 1977).

When put on a optimism-pessimism scale, one could say that the first conclusions clearly tend to the pessimistic pole, whereas the fourth rates as fairly neutral and the fifth as clearly optimistic. And as one moves from the pessimistic to the optimistic statements, the mode of language evolves from factual analysis (IS) to statements of hope and belief (OUGHT). We ourselves have furthermore been struck by the fact that the HOPEFUL statements in reports like these nearly always include an appeal to education (both school and adult education) as a saving tool for change.

The 1980s : multiple crisis, new social movements and the debate over alternatives

The time that appeals like those just alluded to would set the hearts and minds of (adult) educators aglow seems to belong to an ill-remembered and foreclosed past. "Formal", i.e. curricular and certificate-oriented education, as well as "nonformal", i.e. general or experiential and free education have, from the end of the seventies onwards, increasingly been viewed as either alienated from or powerless towards a world-in-crisis. The Western version of the "Death-of-the-School" Movement, initiated by I. Illich and the Cuernavaca-group, tried to make it clear that the institutionalized school had no future and they pleaded for bringing education back to society and real life in a kind of open network system. It is interesting to note that Russia has also known its "Death-of-the-School" Movement, strongly criticizing the separation of education from labour and pleading for close integration. Adult education, as far as it is administered by professionally led institutions, has equally come under heavy attack in several countries. Thus the Dutch philosopher H. Achterhuis (ACHTERHUIS, 1981) spoke of the "market of well-being and happiness", meaning hereby the institutionalized world of welfare and education, which not only exerts in his view, a purely reproductive function in a (neo)capitalist society, but also takes away the citizen's capacity to take care of his own life and puts the responsibility in the hands of professional "change agents" or "caretakers of wellbeing". Only informal, spontaneous (self)education embedded in everyday life finds grace in the eyes of some critics of the educational system.

Even if adult education were to be de-institutionalized and de-professionalized, one may wonder whether the central goal of adult education - to enable adults to get a better insight into their personal and societal situation and to provide them with skills to act upon that situation - would in the long run be better realized.

The UNESCO-Conferences on adult education from 1972 to 1985, and especially the 1976 Declaration of Nairobi, have made it clear that there is not only a great need for a better integration of and more cooperation between all educational systems but also that adult education is confronted with a world-in-multiple crisis, and has both to gain a critical insight into that crisis and possible alternative solutions, and enable adults to learn essential life skills. The latter element has strongly been stressed in R. Faure's eloquent <u>Apprendre à Etre - Learning to be</u> (FAURE, 1971).

The question must be asked however whether theoreticians and practitioners of adult education have had both the opportunity and the courage to reach an in-depth insight both into the dimensions of the multiple world-crisis and into the alternative solutions put forward in the past ten years. We cannot indeed content ourselves with quick references to the employment, environment, or nuclear arms race crises, to the North-South rift or to the upsurge of new technologies.

Neither can we still our concern by indulging in descriptive analyses of educational enterprises in the problem areas just described, or by developing pure theoretical models of, for example, environmental education or peace education. Without denying the legitimacy of such efforts we wish to stress the need to give our thorough and continuous attention to comprehensive and in-depth analyses of major developments from the (recent) past towards the foreseeable future.

In the recent past, we have been confronted with several such analyses, either global or aspectual. Let us point here to the works of K. Boulding (BOULDING, 1968), K. Galbraith (GALBRAITH, 1958), I. Illich (ILLICH, 1978), and, in our own Netherlandic-speaking area, of J. Tinbergen (TINBERGEN, 1970) and L. Baeck (BAECK, 1985).

Most of these works combine the power of analysis with the power of vision, yet, as T.R. Gurr (GURR, 1985) has remarked, they almost inevitably lacked in precision of assumptions based on solid data and in concreteness of a strategy for the future. Yet, they provided us with powerful metaphors, like K. Boulding's contrast between the growth mania of the open "cowboy economy" versus the ecologically oriented "spaceman economy" that should guide the "spaceship earth".

In the wake of the Club of Rome reports, the spectrum of analysis was broadened to larger ecological studies of both quantitative and qualitative nature, which were either optimistic like those by S. Stavrianos (STAVRIANOS, 1976), B. Lovins (LOVINS,

1977) or J. Galtung (GALTUNG, 1983), or pessimistic like those by R.L. Heilbronner (HEILBRONNER, 1974) or D. Meadows (MEADOWS, et al., 1972). Ecological optimists, says Gurr, may be right in the short run and the global aggregate but they may be wrong in the long run, especially if one includes the political perspective : "just as there are ultimate ecological constraints in economic growth, political constraints weigh heavily on what might be achieved collectively in the face of serious scarcity" (GURR, 1985, p.59). Facing a situation of growing scarcity and ecological constraints, the modern state has developed two alternative strategies : either the growth-regenerating strategy of stimulating investments and technological innovation, or the strategy of adapting to ecological constraints, either in a limited sense of redistribution of the costs of scarcity over different social groups, or in the sense of a comprehensive strategy of "deliberate scarcities" and social control. One of the most interesting efforts in this direction has been undertaken by H. Daly (DALY, 1980), persistent and lucid advocate of the so called steady-state economy.

Daly and his co-authors not only tackle the problem of the economic crisis, but put it in a broad ecological and ethical perspective. They thus join a trend that has become popular with "concerned scientists", who cross disciplinary borders and integrate their specialized knowledge within a broader, often morally oriented framework. We want to briefly present here Daly's poignant criticism of the growth paradigm, the broad spectrum of ends-and-means, and the controversial but concrete program for the future.

> Thus, continual growth in both capacity (stock) and income (flow) is a central part of the neoclassical growth paradigm. But in a finite world continual growth is impossible. Given finite stomachs, finite lifetimes, and the kind of man who does not live by bread alone, growth becomes undesirable long before it becomes impossible. But the tacit, and sometimes explicit, assumption of the Keynesian-neoclassical growth mania synthesis is that aggregate wants are infinite and should be served by trying to make aggregate production infinite, and that technology is an omnipotent 'deus ex machina' who will get us out of any growth-induced problems (DALY, 1980, p.5).

Adult Education

What we need, therefore, is a shift of scientific and social paradigm, which will enable us to answer questions like those formulated by the A.A.A.S. (Am. Association for the Advancement of Science) in 1977 :

1. How to live on a <u>finite earth</u> ?
2. How to live <u>a good life</u> on a finite earth ?
3. How to live a good life on a finite earth <u>at peace and without destructive mismatches</u> ?

The answers to questions like these can only be found when we re-order both scientific inquiry and social practice along an integrated ends-means spectrum, an example of which is visualized in the following diagram :

Figure 1.4

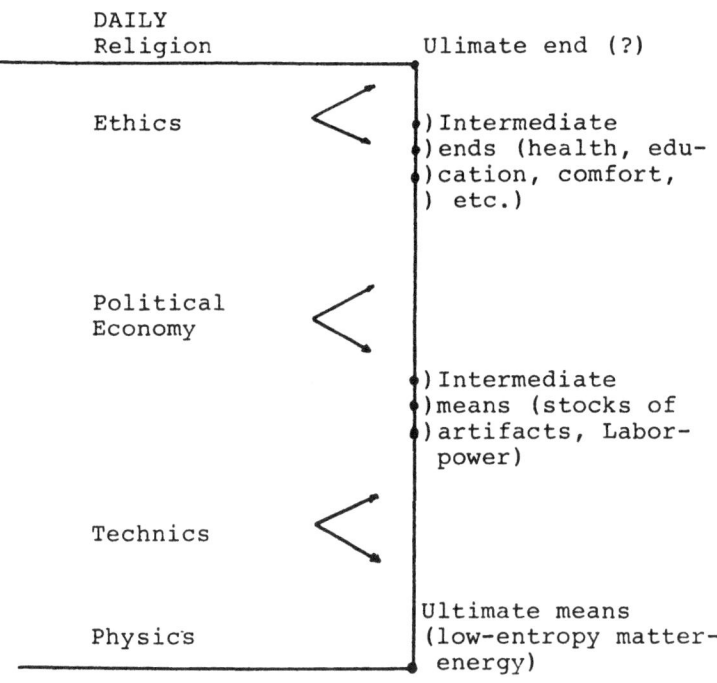

Ends-means spectrum

At the bottom of the spectrum, we find <u>ultimate means</u>, i.e. the "useful stuff of the world" or, in more scientific terms, <u>low-entropy matter-energy</u>, which we can only use up and cannot create or replenish, and whose net production, therefore, cannot be the end of human activity. At the top of the spectrum, we have the <u>Ultimate End</u> - that which is intrinsically good, the existence of which we are logically forced to recognize, but have a lasting difficulty to define. Between both poles, we have intermediate categories, which are of a double nature : they are <u>means</u> to the higher ends above them, and <u>ends</u> to the means below them. Thus health is a means to the ultimate good, but it is an end to such intermediate means as labour-power. At the left of the spectrum, the "traditional disciplines" are given their relative place. We shall immediately return to this construct.

A consideration of the ultimate poles of the spectrum forces us to ask two questions :

1. What, precisely, are our ultimate means, and are they limited in ways that cannot be overcome by technology ?
2. What is the nature of the Ultimate End, and is it such that, beyond a certain point, further accumulation of intermediate means ... not only fails to serve the Ultimate End, but actually renders a disservice ?

The group of authors who, coming from different disciplines, analyze the relationship between <u>economics, ecology and ethics</u>, argue that the answer to both questions is <u>yes</u>.

Even if we basically accept the argument as presented here, we are left wondering how the world and its several regions are to reach the goal of human and ecological equilibrium ? Phrased very briefly, Daly's answer is that we should install three social institutions of control :

1. minimum and maximum limits of income and a maximum on individual wealth, which would help create a more just world order;
2. a transferable birth license of 2.1 children per woman, which would allow zero population growth;
3. depletion quotas for all non-renewable resources, such as oil or coal, which would

safeguard biophysical equilibrium.

To those who would shove such proposals aside as merely utopian, T.R. Gurr answers that a country like China offers the most notable living example of a political system committed to the dual principles of material equality and frugality, which has in fact implemented the first two of the three institutions just mentioned. On the other hand, one should not forget that national planning and strong political control are essential characteristics of the Chinese strategy (GURR, 1985, p.68).

Let us now return to the ends-means spectrum described above. As we can see, education is seen here as an intermediate end, something worth striving for, expressed in popular statements like "everyone should get a good education" or in more solemn Declarations of Human Rights or in statements of educational policy. When we look to the left of the spectrum, we see that the "traditional" disciplines dealing with such human goods are "ethics" and "political economy". Without denying the legitimacy of such a relationship, and without blaming an economist too heavily for the omission, we wish to point out that several other disciplines have for nearly a century been dealing with the middle section of the spectrum, such as psychology, sociology, anthropology and the educational sciences, of which adult education is a part. The omission is a revealing one, certainly in the case of the educational sciences.

From outside this discipline, education is primarily seen as enlightened practice. We found yet another example of this in the penetrating study of "World Environmental Trends Between 1972 and 1982" made for the United Nations Environment Programme (UNEP). The final conclusion of this report reads as follows : "Fourth and perhaps of overwhelming importance, education, training and the development of social strategies for application of available scientific knowledge practically on the ground and especially in developing regions is of paramount importance - and is indeed probably the major environmental need in the world at the present time" (HOLDGATE et al., 1982, p.27).

But from within, (adult) educationists have to ask themselves whether they have made valid contributions towards the construction and implementation of educative programs in the existential problem areas of our time. My personal impression, based on field explorations in Europe and North America and on an analysis of (a part of) the literature, is that we are not yet adequately meeting the challenges of our times : there is, on the one hand, too much engagement based on slogans and superficial knowledge, and on the other hand, too much theorizing without solid roots in practice.

Towards a social-communicative paradigm for an ecological man-world education ?
Our brief necessary side-step into the multiple world-crisis and the search for possible solutions brings us back now to the practice and the science of education. "Education for survival" and "Survival learning" have become leading notions on the educative world-scene. To the middle and young generations of the Northern Hemisphere this is a relatively new and painful experience, and in this respect they can learn many a lesson from their counterparts of the Southern Hemisphere, at least from those who belong to the "culture of silence" and are trying to better their life conditions.

Looking at the future of adult education from a historical perspective, R. Boshier (BOSHIER, 1979) states that in different epochs of the past, the pendulum of adult education has been swinging back and forth between a learner-centred and a societal-centred goal orientation. By learner-centred he means an educational activity "where the starting point and long-term goal... concerns the need and desire to facilitate the self-actualization of individual learners". Such activity has generally only an indirect impact on society as a whole. On the other hand, societal-centred adult education "is conducted because education can be instrumental in ameliorating or changing some social condition or problem. The condition may be small - such as the need for townspeople to learn how to use a new water supply - or large - such as the need for an entire nation to learn how to cope with radio-active wastes". (BOSHIER, 1979, p.180) The author further notes that a specific educational program may have a high or a (rather) low utility, for either the individual or the society viz. the community. To him, the desired future would be one where learner orientation and societal orientation are combined, with a high utility to both. The community and action programs promulgated by Freire and his collaborators provide a good example of this combination, as well as the Nicaraguan Literacy and Basic Education Program between 1979 and 1985 or - closer to our own situation - a number of so-called Open School or Open University programs for adults in countries like Great Britain and the Netherlands.

The likely future seems to be one, however, where societal needs will be met to a high degree, but with a low utility to a large group of individual learners. We might call this survival learning for society's sake.

In retrospect, the situation of the "golden sixties" tended towards the opposite : it looked like welfare learning for individuals with a restricted utility for society.

One of the major challenges to the discipline as well as to the field of adult education in the near future is the (further) development of concepts, strategies, methods and materials for both learner- and society-oriented education in vital areas like labour and (un)employment, environmental care, housing, national and international conflict, the relationship between so-called developed and developing nations, the use and abuse of new technologies...

We have just noted that the field of adult education has, generally speaking, shown a shift from learner-oriented to societal-oriented goals and programs in the past two decades.

Our retrospective tale of the evolution of the scientific discipline up to the mid-seventies likewise indicated a clear shift both in paradigms and in research methodologies. In this respect, the discipline of (adult)education merely followed a general trend. The phenomenon of abrupt paradigmatic change was systematically analyzed in 1969 by Th. Kuhn (KUHN, 1962) with relation to the physical sciences, and then extended to the behavioral and/or social sciences by P. Lakatos (LAKATOS, 1970) and I. Feyerabend (FEYERABEND, 1970).

A short while ago, we have ourselves analyzed the evolution of theory building and research in adult education in Benelux, based inter alia on a study of one of our research assistants (LEIRMAN, 1985). We later found the basic lines of that analysis confirmed and broadened in an article by Horst Ruprecht, covering the evolution in Germany (RUPRECHT, 1981).

In the mid-sixties, the predominant paradigm of educational science was of an empirical-analytical nature, based on a behavioural definition of learning and on a concept of education as an observable process that would bring the learner from stated goals towards measurable new knowledge, new attitudes and new skills. The research cycle usually followed was called <u>predictive</u>, starting with a general theory or theoretical proposition, which was then operationalized into a (set of) research hypothesis(es) and put to the test in conditions that had to be directly or indirectly controlled. Careful analysis of the data then allowed the (non) verification of the initial hypothesis and the underlying theory. If this could not be achieved - as was regularly the case in educational settings - researchers had to resort to descriptive or exploratory studies, which would eventually lead to the desired goal of predictive empirical research. Overviews of adult education research (like the one by E. Brunner (BRUNNER, 1961)) as well as research conference programs of that epoch indeed reveal that this was the dominant trend. We may point here to research into the variables that determined (non)participation, (see the pioneering work of C. Verner (VERNER and BOOTH, 1964)), into the effects of programs and into the motives of adult learners.

By the mid-seventies, an alternative approach came to the forefront, which has been given different names : hermeneutical or interpretative, normative-critical, social-communicative. It was based on a more qualitative concept of learning and adult education - in the sense of the definitions given above. Education was seen as a process based in the existential needs of "participants" which would eventually lead to a more critical insight and increased personal and social action skills. Within this paradigm, two related research cycles have been developed. One can be called <u>interpretative</u>, starting with an exploration of the life-world or the thematic universe, and moving via a codification of experiences and needs towards their interpretation or decodification and the consideration of possible solutions. The second one has been called <u>regulative</u> or action-oriented, since it does not restrict itself to reflection and communication, but combines the reflexive operations of the interpretative cycle with the action-oriented steps of planning, execution and evaluation.

The hallmark of both these cycles is the social-communicative orientation, where the researcher does not take the stand of a distant observer or of a cool experimenter, but engages in a dialogue with and becomes a virtual member of the existential world he will try to understand "from within". The action-oriented approach, however, may shift from a "soft" communicative strategy to a "hard" power strategy.

The (meta)theoretical base for this approach has been delivered by social-oriented scientists like A. Giddens (GIDDENS, 1976), A. Peukert (PEUKERT, 1978) and especially J. Habermas (HABERMAS, 1981) in his theory of the communicative act.

Early examples of this approach are to be found in anthropological studies of so-called foreign cultures or in the works of Kurt Lewin (LEWIN, 1948) and initial group dynamics research. By the end of the seventies, especially in Latin America and in Europe, adult education research projects often bore a basic social-communicative direction, leading to a better insight into educational needs and motives, into concrete models for diagnosis and methods of community education, and into the conditions under which adults learn to overcome threatening life situations. An important contribution to the latter area was made by M. Gronemeyer (GRONEMEYER, 1976) who, on the basis of concrete cases such as the "citizens' action" against the planned nuclear centre of Wyhl in south-west Germany, developed a theory of political learning and dissipated the idea that crisis situations such as unemployment and its concomitant phenomena of psychological isolation and shrinking social contacts provide of themselves the motivation for social (re)action and change. From her point of view, she states that "the unlimited accumulation of quantitative and alienated needs can only be prevented and stopped by one kind of process : the development of qualitative needs" (GRONEMEYER, 1981, p. 141). Such a development is only possible when gratifying counter-experiences can be made, like "knowing how good it does to decide for oneself" and to "engage in competition-free social contacts". Yet this and other promising onsets cannot prevent us from stating that the step towards a fully-fledged theory of environmental or peace competency education still has to be made.

The description of the shift from one dominant paradigm to another within the timespan of two decades might suggest that we are facing here a complete antithesis. This suggestion is enforced by the small or big conflicts between "schools of thought" that have been and are still being waged. However we sincerely doubt whether that is true.

On the other hand, we would be scientifically

and socially naive if we were to state that an integration of both global approaches can easily be reached. As several commentators have remarked, differences in paradigms refer to different underlying metatheories as well as to different normative visions. Both have their merits and their legitimacy, as well as their limitations. And both may become ideologies that will alienate us from man and the world.

The discipline of adult education has gained much from the empirical-analytical tradition. Our insight into dimensions and phases of the educative process, into psychological and social conditions of learning, into the illusion of quick attitude change, into the nature of systems and subsystems of education, into leadership styles and their effects into the diffusion of knowledge, into the effects of new technologies, etc. has largely been acquired thanks to this tradition.

Yet, we share the conviction of many educationists that the qualitative goals of education as well as the multiple world-crisis situation forces us to invest much of our attention and energy into the further development of the social-communicative paradigm.

At the beginning of our general introduction, we referred to the parable of the grasshopper and the owl. Given the evolution of two decades, we might add a sequel or even a counter-parable, as follows :

> At the end of the next winter, a group of grasshoppers came back to see master owl. He was delighted to notice that they looked rather well, and he asked them : "Well, did you apply my principle?" One grasshopper, apparently the leader of the group replied : "No sir. We held a long discussion, and then decided to build a shelter with the means at hand." "That may well be," said the owl, "but I do not see the principle behind all this." The leader smilingly replied : "To understand this, you will have to come off your branch, and to share our grassroots experience. Good principles are learned from good practice ...".

The solution of the existential problems of our times - or positively stated, the transition towards biophysical equilibrium and a more just and peaceful world - will certainly not be brought about by edu-

Adult Education

cation alone, or even primarily by education. On the other hand, some adherents of new social movements state that their massive and continued efforts will bring about the desired changes. A look at the anti-missile peace movement in Western Europe shows that such a statement cannot generally be upheld, even though other movements, like the environmental movement, have been able to realize changes in both

Figure 1.5

A sequel to the parable of the owl and the grasshopper : "good principles evolve from good practice ..."

mentality and political decision making in different regions of the world. Still other analysts proclaim that only the accumulation of dramatic events and structural interventions by old or new social elites can provoke lasting social change. A reference to popular movements such as those led by Martin Luther King, Mahatma Gandhi or to Solidarnosc in Poland may serve as a reminder that structural intervention is not the universal lever to social change. It is our conviction that combinations of formal and informal education will be needed to meet the challenges of the near future, as has been the case in similar world-crisis situations. For our country, we can refer to the educative actions of Joseph Cardijn and his collaborators among young Christian labourers in the years 1920-1930, which later inspired a world-wide movement.

The further development of a social-communicative paradigm in adult education, with an adequate use of empirical-analytical methods, basically implies the combination of three lines of action :

1. the continuing analysis of the bio-social context on the macro- and meso-levels <u>and</u> of the life-world of individuals and social groups ; we thereby will have to rely on the help of and the cooperation with several other disciplines;
2. the development or further refining of models and strategies of general and specific ecological man-world education, based on field studies and on self-initiated projects;
3. the pre- and in-service training of both researchers and practitioners of adult education in the types of analysis and educative action we have specified above.

To carry out such a program in the "iron eighties" and the yet un-defined nineties, we will need both insight, skilful action and courage. Within our own university, we have found continual inspiration in the example of several colleagues, not least in that of our former rector, the late Prof. P. De Somer. His critical analysis and condemnation of the nuclear arms race in 1983 was one example of a scientist who knew how to combine academic freedom with social responsibility (DE SOMER, 1983). We hope the contributions presented here will reveal the same qualities.

REFERENCES

Achterhuis, H. (1981) *De markt van welzijn en geluk*, Ambo, Baar

Aspeslagh, R., Vriens, L.J.A. and Son, G. (eds) (1981) *Pedagogiek voor de vrede. Opvoeden tegen de stroom in*, Vredesopbouw Utrecht, Utrecht

Baeck, L. (1985) *Macht en tegenmacht. Een sociopolitieke visie op de wereld.*, Davidsfonds, Leuven

Baert, H. (1983) 'Agogische draagkracht. Een aanzet tot operationele begripsbepaling', *Tijdschrift voor Agologie*, 12, 5-23

Ballauff, Th. (1958) *Erwachsenenbildung - Sinn und Grenzen*, Quelle und Meyer

Bennis, W.G., Benne, K.D. and Chin, R. (eds) (1961) *The planning of change*, Holt, Rinehart and Winston, New York, London

Boshier, R.W. (1979) *Adult education : Issues of the Future*, UBC, Vancouver

Boulding, K. (1968) *Beyond economics : essays on society, religion and ethics*, Univ. of Michigan Press, Ann Arbor

Brunner, E. (ed.) (1967) *An overview of adult education research*, Adult Ed. Assoc. of U.S.A., Washington

Burch, W.R. (1979) *Readings in Ecology, Energy, and Human Society : Contemporary Perspectives*, Harper and Row, New York etc.

Cacérès, B. (1964) *Histoire de l'éducation populaire*, Ed. du Seuil, Paris

Daly, H. (ed.) (1980) *Economics, Ecology, Ethics*, W.H. Freeman, San Francisco

De Somer, P. (1983) *Reflecties omtrent kernbewapening*, K.U.L., Leuven

Dickinson, C., Leirman, W., Niskala, H., and Verner, C. (1970) *The preparation of adult educators. A selected review of the literature produced in North America*, ERIC, New York

Faure, E. (ed.) (1971) *Apprendre à être. Learning to be*, UNESCO, Paris

Feyerabend, P. (1970) 'Against Method : an outline of an anarchistic theory of knowledge' in H. Feigl and G. Maxwell (eds), *Minnesota studies in the philosophy of science*, Minneapolis, vol. IV, 17-130

Freire, P. (1970) *Pedagogia del Oprimido*, Tierra Nueva, Montevideo (transl. into English, French, German, Netherlandic)

Galbraith, K. (1958) *The affluent society*, Houghton Mifflin, Boston

Galtung, J. (1983) There are alternatives. Four ways to peace and security, Stockholm
Gelpi, E. (1982) 'Education permanente : créativités et résistances', Paidea, 11, 227-87
Giddens, A. (1976) New rules of sociological method, Hutchinson, London
Gids Sociaal-Cultureel Werk, o.v.w. De Bock, G., Foubert, J., Leirman, W., Raes, B., Roels, R. (1981), Van Loghum Slaterus, Antwerpen, 3 vol. (contin. series)
Giesecke, H. (1973) Bildungsreform und Emanzipation, Juventa, München
Gronemeyer, M. (1976) Motivation und politisches Handeln. Grundkategorien politischer Psychologie, Hoffmann und Campe
Gronemeyer, M. (1981) Lebenlernen unter dem Zwang der Krise? in H.E. Bahr and R. Gronemeyer (eds), Anders leben - überleben, Fischer, Frankfurt, 113-48
Gurr, T.R. (1985) 'On the political consequences of scarcity and economic decline', International Studies Quarterly, 29, 51-75
Habermas, J. (1970) Technik und Wissenschaft als Ideologie, Suhrkamp, Frankfurt
Habermas, J. (1981) Theorie des kommunikativen Handelns,
I. Handlungsrationalität und gesellschaftliche Rationalisierung
II. Zur Kritik der funktionalistischen Vernunft
Suhrkamp, Frankfurt, 2 vol.
Heilbronner, R.L. (1974) An inquiry into the human prospect
Hinnekint, H. (1985) 'De vierde Unesco-wereldconferentie over volwasseneneducatie', Vorming Vlaanderen, 1, nr. 1, 32-54
Holdgate, M.W., Kassas, M. and White, G.F. (1982) 'World Environmental trends between 1972 and 1982' (Synthesis of UNEP-report), Environmental Conversation, 9, n°1, 11-29
Holdgate, M.W., Kassas, M., White, G.F. (1983) The world environment 1972-1982. A report by the United Nations Environment Programme, Tycooly, Dublin
Houle, C. (1961) The inquiring mind, Univ. of Wisconsin Press, Madison
Illich, I. (1978) Towards a history of needs, Pantheon, New York
Johnstone and Rivera (1965) Volunteers for learning Aldine, Chicago
Knoll, J. (1968) 'Ausserschulische Pädagogik als

Wissenschaft von der Erwachsenenbildung' in C. Ritters (ed.), Theorien der Erwachsenenbildung, Beltz, Weinheim, 70-86
Knowles, M.S. (1970) The modern practice of adult education. Andragogy versus pedagogy, Association Press, New York
Kuhn, Th. (1962) The structure of scientific revolutions, Univ. of Chicago Press, Chicago
Lakatos, I. (1970) The changing logic of scientific discovery, Cambr. Univ. Press, Cambridge
Leirman, W. and Pöggeler, F. (eds) (1979) Erwachsenenbildung in fünf Kontinenten, Kohlhammer, Stuttgart
Leirman, W. and Vandemeulebroecke, L. (eds) (1981) (1984) Vormingswerk en vormingswetenschap, Een agalogisch handboek.,
I. Achtergrondvragen en uitgangspunten
II. Het vormingsproces
Helicon, Leuven, 2 vol.
Leirman, W. (1985) 'Recente ontwikkelingen in de vormingswetenschap', Pedagogisch Tijdschrift, 10, 282-94
Lengrand, P. (1966) L'éducation permanente, Peuple et Culture, Paris
Lewin, K. (1948) Resolving social conflicts, Harper, New York
Lippitt, R., Watson, J. and Westley, R. (1958) The dynamics of planned change, Harcourt, Brace and World, New York
Lovins, B. (1977) Soft energy paths : toward a durable peace, Penguin, Harmondsworth
Masschelein, J. '(Ped)agogisch handelen als communicatief handelen?' in W. Leirman and L. Vandemeulebroecke (eds), Vormingswerk en vormingswetenschap, vol. II, 107-29
Meadows, D.L. et al. (ed.) (1972) The limits to growth. A report for the Club of Rome's project on the predicament of mankind, Universe, New York
Meadows, D.L. (1977) 'The predicament of mankind' in W. Burch (ed.), Readings in Ecology, 209-16
Mollenhauer, K. (1970) Erziehung und Emanzipation, Juventa, Munchen
Nuttin, J. (1974) Psychoanalyse en persoonlijkheid, Scriptoria, Antwerpen (transl. in Engl.)
Peukert, A. (1978) Wissenschaftstheorie. Handlungstheorie. Fundamentele Theologie, Suhrkamp, Darmstadt
Pöggeler, F. (1957) Einführung in die Andragogik, Henn, Ratingen

Pöggeler, F. and Wolterhoff, B. (eds) (1981) Neue Theorien der Erwachsenenbildung, Kohlhammer, Stuttgart
Rogers, E. and Shoemaker, F. (1971) Communications of innovations. A crosscultural approach, The Free Press, New York
Röling, B.V.A. (1981) Vredeswetenschap. Een inleiding tot de polemologie, Spectrum, Utrecht-Antwerpen
Ruprecht, H. (1981) 'Über den Zusammenhang von Forschungsmethoden im Feld der Erwachsenenbildung' in F. Pöggeler (ed.), Neue Theorien der Erwachsenenbildung, 112-28
Salgado, J. (1985) Alfabetisación en America Latina en su contexto internacional. Estudio comparado de los casos de Brasil, Chile, Mexico y Nicaragua, Kath. Univ., Fac. Psych. and Ed. Sc., Leuven, 2 vol. (doct. diss.)
Schwartz, B. (1977) Une autre école, Flammarion, Paris
Stalpers, J.A. (1981) 'Van een verzorgingsstaat naar een zorgende samenleving' in W. Leirman and L. Vandemeulebroecke, Vormingswerk en vormingswetenschap, vol. I, 117-31
Stavrianos, S. (1981) The promise of the coming dark, New York
Stretton, H. (1976) Capitalism, socialism and the environment, Cambr. Univ. Press, Cambridge
Ten Have, T.T. (1976) Andragogie, een terreinverkenning, Tjeenk Willink, Groningen
Ten Have, T.T. (1973) Andragologie in blauwdruk Tjeenk Willink, Groningen
Tinbergen, J. (1970) Een leefbare aarde, Elsevier, Amsterdam-Brussel
Verner, C. and Booth, A. (1964) Adult education, Library of Education, New York
Von Werder, L. (1980) Alltägliche Erwachsenenbildung. Aspekte einer bügernahen Pädagogik, Beltz, Weinheim-Basel
Weinstein, C.E. and Mayer, R.E. (1982) The teaching of learning strategies, Univ. of Texas, Austin (manuscript for Handbook of Research on Teaching, Third Ed.)
Wehr, P. (1979) (1981) Conflict Regulation, Westview Press, Boulder Co.
Welten, V.J. et al. (1973) Jeugd en emancipatie. Voorstudie voor een empirisch onderzoek, Ambo, Bilthoven
Wildemeersch, D. (1985) Ruimtelijke ordening in het perspectief van vorming en samenlevingsopbouw,

Adult Education

   Kath. Univ., Fac. Psych. and Ed. Sc., Leuven,
   (doct. dissert.)

Chapter Two
PRODUCTIVITY AND TIME: A REFLECTION ABOUT THE FUTURE

Tamas PALASTHY
University of Louvain-La-Neuve (1)
Belgium

Introduction
One should search for a certain coherence behind the rumour of every-day events. This coherence can be found in the goals pursued simultaneously in search for 'survival'. Within the context of a growing interdependence, their actions and reactions are reflected in the fluctuations of the level of economic activity of all regions in the world.
    In the following pages we will try to clarify the most important factors which determine these dependencies, in order to situate the West in a world-wide context. As we shall see the solutions to the present crisis depend essentially on a fundamental political choice concerning the future organisation of society, because this is the only adjustable internal factor in the West.

1. Basic principles
Economic performance and social performance within one region cannot be mixed up. The economic growth of a region is measured by the degree of variations in the time of the actual demand or, in other words, of the level of economic activity.
    On the other hand the difference between the potential demand and the actual demand of the households constitutes the standard of the global social performance of a region. For this reason it is correct to use the common term 'social progress' to denote this decreasing difference, and the term 'social regression' to denote this increasing difference.
    The main factors which, in an interdependent way, determine the actual demand or, in other words, the level of economic activity are :

1. the number, the demographic structure, the degree of knowledge, the dynamism, etc. ... of the population;
2. the social organisation;
3. the volume and the productivity of the available production-infrastructure;
4. the availability of natural resources, renewable and unrenewable;
5. the climatological and topographic conditions.

Within a perspective of the maintenance of the activity level, any modification of one of these factors which affects the economic activity level in a negative way, should automatically bring forth an adjustment through a growing mobilisation of one or several factors.

The more a region is open towards the external world (2), the more its economic activity level will depend on the variations of the same factors in other regions. The external relations are not limited to the trade exchange (actually the external trade); they also include the transfers of capital, the population migrations and the exchange and transfer of knowledge. While the trade exchange directly influences the level of economic activity, via the exchange terms, the other kind of relations modify it indirectly by means of the available internal factors. Besides, the evolution of the potential demand is also conditioned by the migration patterns and the exchange and transfer of knowledge. If in this context, the interregional and international traffic reduces the social performance, the adjustment of the social organisation becomes inevitable, to prevent the region from losing its socio-economic coherence.

This adjustment necessitates either a reduction of the degree of openness (protectionism), or the modification of the rules that determine the expansion of the potential demands and the actual demand.

The social performance of a region thus partly depends on internal factors, and partly on external factors, in relation to its degree of openness towards the external world. This is the reason why, in the case of a manifest social regression, three questions arise automatically :

1. To what extent is the regression due to external factors ?

2. To what extent can one act upon these factors in order to adjust the evolution ?
3. What can be the consequences of a partial or a failing adjustment ?

An answer to these questions necessitates in the first place an analysis of the important tendencies that determine the interregional and international relations.

2. Important tendencies
All regions in the world are more or less open towards the external world and are thus part of the interdependent relationships. This implies that the potential demand and the level of economic activity are everywhere conditioned by the following important tendencies :

1. the continuous growth of the world-wide potential demand;
2. the convergence of the regional prices;
3. the almost exponential growth of the knowledge production.

These three tendencies or movements, which are a source of profit for the enterprises in a market economy, can be considered as primary.
There are two other important, though secondary tendencies :

1. the growing intervention of the public authorities in the social organisation;
2. the fluctuation of the exchange rates due to a drifting monetary system.

These secondary tendencies are to a certain extent the product of the primary tendencies. They reflect the efforts of the public and the monetary authorities in search for a solution to the economic evolution which is restrained by a conjunction of tendencies.

The continuous growth of the world-wide potential demand
The United Nations predict a doubling of the world's population between 1900 and 2100. Following the logic of a logistic growth, the population will grow from 1.3 milliard to 3 milliard inhabitants. At the present moment we are going through the ascendant

stage of this logistic growth. Consequently the actual number of inhabitants will double by the end of the next forty years. The population will thus grow from 4.3 milliard to 9 milliard inhabitants.

If we wish to maintain the present standard of living, production must necessarily follow the natural growth of the world's population. Apart from this evolution, the human expectations also rise under the influence of schooling, mass-media messages and travelling behaviour (business travelling, tourism, etc. ...).

Demographic growth, together with rising expectations, will thus create an unbridled increase of the potential demand. The present growth of the worldwide production is insufficient or even ridiculously small, to meet this demand. The outbursts of social tensions over the world illustrate this discrepancy.

Thus, the growth of the potential demand in relation to the actual demand is a source of social tension. At the same time this combination is a source of social profit as it stimulates enterprises to organise future production. This results in a world-wide growth of the demand of production factors. In its turn this evolution influences the price of these factors. The effects can be summed up as follows :

1. The <u>real rate of interest</u> reaches a very high level as the demand of capital surpasses the supply of capital. In fact, the supply of real capital is totally inelastic in this case.
2. The <u>rent</u> to be paid for the use of natural resources increases as a consequence of the excessive demand, while the supply of natural resources is very inelastic in the medium run.
3. The <u>ways</u> remain unvariable or even show a decreasing trend. Indeed, the labour-demand increases but is surpassed by the labour supply, due to the demographic growth and rising expectation towards a better standard of living.

In relation to this inelasticity of the supply of material means of production (capital, natural resources), the response given to the growth of potential demand is seriously inhibited, because of the absorption of the profit margin due to the rising prices of these means. Even in the 'dirigistic' countries the main obstacle to a production growth is the increasing scarcity of material means of production.

The consequences of the increasing world-wide potential demand are roughly :

1. that relative "world" prices of the production factors are constantly modified in relation to the scarcity of the material means of production and the relative labour-surplus. Consequently the wages decrease in relation to the interest and the rent;
2. that the modification of the relative prices for the production factors implies ipso facto the modification of the repartition of the result of the production process (income);
3. that the modification of the repartition which brings about social tensions or even social conflicts, necessitates changes in social organisation.

These findings bring us to the conclusion that the continuous growth of the potential demand is one of the important tendencies for the future, because this growth will everywhere condition the level of economic activity, unless the borders are completely closed or a catastrophe occurs.

Convergence of regional prices
The disparities, among the several regions, of the internal factors that condition the level of economic activity, are important. These disparities are reflected into the system of the relative prices, including the price for the production factors. The employee-salaries, for instance, are ten times higher in the developed countries than in some countries of the Third World.

These disparities are a source of profit for the enterprises who try to reduce them : indeed, the international and interregional exchanges, the transfers of funds and the re-localisation of the production, are a product of these disparities; but at the same time the traffic guarantees the convergence of all regional prices. Moreover the disparities among the real wages induce the migrations of populations in search for a better standard of living.

Productivity and Time

The velocity of the convergence of prices depends both upon the degree of the disparities and the natural and social obstacles obstructing the international traffic of people, goods and information.

The continuous diminution of transport cost, of communications and distant management progressively take away the influence of national obstacles (distances, topography, ...)

The obstacles with a social character however still have an important influence and moreover, they often vary in relation to the political necessities for the time being. Thus, the convergence rate depends in the first place on the attitude of the countries in the world towards the freedom of the international traffic of people, goods and information (what is called erroneously : free-exchange). From this point of view we can classify the countries into three categories :

1. the countries favourable to a liberalisation of the international traffic; this group is essentially composed of Third World countries;
2. the countries opposed to this traffic; this group is essentially composed of the 'communist' countries;
3. the countries with an intermediate position; this group is essentially composed of the Western countries (Western Europe, North-America, Japan).

Indeed the Third World countries and to some extent the industries of the developed countries, can take considerable profit from the convergence of prices in case of an exchange-liberalisation. On the other hand, many industries and the majority of the population of the Western countries would be worse off : the growing competition in the rest of the world, enhanced by the traffic of production will rather reduce the rentability of Western production and consequently of employment. This will, in its turn, reduce the spending power of the internal market and by consequence the rentability of local production.

If social obstacles obstructing international traffic are relieved, the halving of the real wages in the Western countries becomes inevitable. This would be the result of the equalising effect of the convergence of regional prices. Indeed, the whole burden will be carried by the West because the Soviet bloc will remain a closed bloc. This is why the tendential convergence of regional prices will remain a highly important political problem (North-South, East-West). The solution to this problem becomes even more complicated due to the debts of the Third World.

Quasi-exponential growth of knowledge
The production, diffusion and application of knowledge has always been a source of profit to the entrepreneurs and a source of power to the governments. They have been used either in the struggle against scarcity of material means of production, or to stimulate their growth.

Today the growth in the domain of knowledge has reached an exponential growth rate. These are the consequences of this progress :

1. The potential demand is increasing because the diffusion of knowledge stimulates the aspiration; moreover the accumulation of knowledge becomes to a larger extent part of the aspiration, which we consider as positive evolution.
2. The application of new knowledge in the domain of the production of goods and services is fostering the productivity of the equipment (of physical capital).

The estimations of the growth of the productivity of equipment in the domain of raw materials and completed products actually amounts to 5-6%. This implies that production can be doubled over a period of 14 years; the volume of labour is held constant. In case of an unchanged production, the volume of labour will have to be halved. However, as we have noticed earlier, the fruits of a growing physical productivity are largely absorbed by the lowering of the output of nature and by the rising of the real interest rate. In this case there is not much margin left for the labour-factor.

The overcompensation of the negative effects of both tendencies (a growing world-wide potential demand and a convergence of prices) by the growing productivity of the Western industries, which for several reasons (vicinity of the markets, too expensive investments, etc. ...) do not succeed in relocalising their production, stimulates even more both the demand of capital and unemployment.

Growing intervention of the Public Authorities into social organisation

Everywhere in the world social organisation becomes more and more complex and consequently more and more vulnerable. The maintenance of internal coherence necessitates a growing public intervention. Moreover, the social tensions resulting from the divergent evolution of the potential demand and the actual demand, have to be mastered or at least tempered, so as to prevent severe social conflicts. These interventions aim at the adjustment of social organisation to the evolution of internal and external factors which condition the economic activity level. They bring about, in different degree, a modification of the external flux and consequently they affect other regions in the world. Finally these interventions can produce severe economic or even political international tensions. This risk is real as long as the countries are inclined to direct the internal conflicts towards the external world.

The growing role of the Public Authorities also affects the continuous growth of public expenses. The tax-financing of these expenses reduces the supply of capital, whereas the loan needed for deficit spending stimulates the demand. In this way the international interest rate is continuously depending on the needs of Public Authorities. In the present system of a united capital market, the local capital demand is added to the world-wide capital demand. As a large part of this capital is used for contra-productive goals (luxury expenses, excessive ornament, etc. ...) the application of capital not only burdens the evolution of interest rates, but also the use of other natural resources and consequently the regional price-setting.

The great number of more or less sovereign or autonomous policy-making centres (international institutions, state- and regional governments) and the extent of their intervention in social organisation, make the predictions which are necessary for economic calculations, more and more difficult and expensive or even impossible. The feeling of permanent instability which follows from this, obstructs production almost everywhere, as the growing risks are now added to the rising real interest rates.

International monetary instability

Governments and monetary authorities pursue two perfectly contradictory objectives in relation to their monetary policy :

1. the maintenance of internal and external purchasing power (parity) of the national currency;
2. the maintenance or even the stimulation of the internal level of economic activity through a policy of cheap credits. The oscillation between both objectives, under pressure of public opinion, in relation to the monetary policy of several countries and particularly the United States (which holds the referential currency), first of all affect the fluctuations of the international interest rate and exchange rate. These fluctuations, which are reinforced by speculation affect the adjustment of the activity level of almost all regions.

The negative effect of the growth of the international potential demand and also of the convergence of regional prices upon Western economy can only be countered by a monetary policy. The manipulation of the currency though is extremely dangerous because it disorientates political and economic decisions with the help of the monetary illusion and the speculation that follows from it. In this way, the real solutions to the problems are postponed. While waiting for the better days to come, the whole economy is put out of order.

Adjustment possibilities of the Western economies in relation to the important tendencies

The consequences of these trends for the Western economies are on the one hand the rising of the real interest rate, technical obsolescence and political risks of monetary and commercial nature, on the other hand the deterioration of the exchange relations (the rising of prices of imported raw materials in relation to the prices of the exported completed products) and a loss of markets.

In these circumstances, an improvement of rentability through the growth of production (rationalisation, application of new technologies, etc. ...) is a normal reaction to external pressure, although this results in rising unemployment. Within the Western fiscal and para-fiscal system this everywhere pressurises the public budget-balance and the social security system.

The slowing down of a rough fall of the level of economic activity, following the principle of the "anticyclic deficit" everywhere provokes a quasi exponential growth of internal public debts. However, as we have shown in our analysis of the important tendencies, this is not at all a phenomenon with a cyclic character. As long as the world economy does not realise a necessary inter-temporal and interregional balance, the economic fluctuations in relation to these long-term trends will indeed continue to exist, especially when the intervention of Public and Monetary Authorities are incoherent. This incoherence of course stimulates these fluctuations.

If the degree of openness of the regions in the world remains unchanged, or even increases, the <u>spontaneous adjustment</u> to this evolution will <u>in any case</u> create an increased degree of unemployment in the West. This growth will depend upon the accepted or imposed austerity policy reduction of wages.

Thus, with an unchanged or rising level of aspiration, the current social regression will be accentuated. Social tensions will be the result of this evolution. The mastering of these tensions will necessitate modifications in social organisation (authoritarian policy, dictatorship) because without such measures the social risks will even worsen the financial problems, which in its turn will affect local production in a negative way. The direction of these social tensions towards the external world, under the mark of "external threat" in order to maintain the internal coherence is a strong argument for acceptance of the modification of social organisation.

This spontaneous adjustment will in our opinion raise questions about the democratic regimes. In order to prevent a closure of the frontiers (protectionism) it is necessary to reflect and act simultaneously in four directions :

1. Reorientation of the aspiration towards the consumption and accumulation of immaterial goods which require much available time and little material goods. To put it in John Stuart Mill's words :

   To many people generosity is like a fragile and easily dying plant, not only under pressure of the enemy, but also when there is a lack of food. To many young people this plant soon withers if the activities, peculiar to the imposed situation and to society into which they are thrown, do not support the maintenance of this superior faculty. Mankind bases its superior aspirations, just like it bases its intellectual capacities, when there is no time or opportunity to practise them. People surrender to inferior pleasure, not because they deliberately choose it, but only because this pleasure is the only accessible or the only one that enables them to enjoy life somewhat longer. One may wonder if a man capable of tasting both kinds of pleasures has ever preferred consciously and in cold blood the inferior pleasures; although many people at any age have exhausted themselves to combine both (Utilitarianism, chapter II).

If we want to give the immaterial goods their proper place, it is absolutely necessary to conceive in the first place a highly qualitative pedagogical project which stimulates both reflection upon human condition and 'the act of living' and which diffuses instrumental knowledge. In the second place it will be necessary to share labour because the unemployed have too much leisure while the employed have no time for the consumption of material goods.
2. An increase of the financial productivity of the enterprises with the help of a new type of labour organisation (flexible labour-system) in order to counter-balance the increase of financial costs induced by the long-term trends and the increase of wage costs induced by inevitable resharing of labour. The economical, social and political consequences of a continuing or even growing unemployment indeed are unpredictable. Consequently it is in the interest of all to share employment within the context of a fundamental reorganisation of private and public production, even if this necessitates mutual concessions.
3. Adoption by the West of the Third World debts even if it were only partial, on con-

       dition that the amounts destined for interests and redemption are used for an increase of employment and/or wages in the Third World. These measures, which are far better than protectionist measures, will result in a diminution of the interregional disparities and consequently in a diminution extent pressure upon production and upon the monetary system of the West.
4. Reduction of the international tensions resulting from internal social tensions, because the financial efforts which they imply heavily burden the evolution of the real interest rate and consequently the growth of production needed by real Humanity.

The first two proposals obviously necessitate profound modification of social organisation. Both a spontaneous and a 'rational' adjustment of social organisation to changes in the world are consequently dependent upon a fundamental political choice for the future in the West.

NOTES

    (1) This text is based on a report written by the author in 1985 at the invitation of the Walloon Region.
    (2) The degree of openness depends on the social organisation of the region.

Chapter Three
EDUCATION, PRODUCTION, DEVELOPMENT AND TECHNOLOGICAL INNOVATION

Ettore GELPI
Unesco, Paris
France

The world of labour shocked
In all countries nowadays, the world of labour is shaken. One is less aware of the shocks concerning education, though they are very numerous. The institutional answers - state, employers, trade unions, Ministry of Education and Labour - often are directed at continuity and adjustment of structures, but the dynamics of production reveal the provisional nature of these answers. The young and the adults live either in situations of marginalisation and uncertainty concerning their function and their identity, or they gain rapid promotion.

> The quest for the orderly, external vision characterizes a disorganized mind which cannot cope with the disorder and has become too dependent on the format of literacy (underlying our use of writing, the print and the computer) to provide the illusion of order (PIM, 1985, p. 403).

The issue is the disorder provoked by the evolutions and ruptures of productive and social relationships. This enterprise may ask for education with very rich cultural components and strongly oriented towards theoretical and empirical research, both on the individual and the collective level.
In order to get a clear view on the relationship between individual and social system, three relations are particularly significant : "individual-social classes, men-women, permanence-mutation" (CAPECHI, 1985). When one takes the example of women's working conditions, one can see that women's jobs are more of a tertiary nature, less qualified, characterized by more instable contracts and with

particular forms of employment (HUET, 1985).

The dualism of the labour market and of the educational system has some consequences for the quality of labour : "The quality of labour is not only linked to personal satisfaction, but also to basic issues like the volume of employment, the qualification and training, the evolution of tasks and wages, and the pace of work" (BIT, 1985, p. 207).

The forms of alienation provoked by certain types of labour do not only concern small minorities. This alienation is not necessarily linked to new or ancient technologies, to the level of salaries or to the initial level of education. In order to respond to this alienation, activities of creation must be developed within as well as outside the working place. At the present time we are still far away from these preoccupations. Workers are mainly seen according to their belonging to a certain category of salary group, and not according to the quality of their work.

If there have been some difficulties in planning the need for qualified workers in times of relative scarcity of this kind of labour, this planning has even become more difficult in an era of lack of employment. The crisis of this planning is not limited to the countries with a free market economy, but also reaches the countries with a planned economy (VESITULUTA et al., 1985).

New profiles of researchers, educators, and education policies have to be developed. In fact, the relation between education and labour does not ask for moralism or slogans, but needs persons who know the evolving reality of production. This entails the necessity of a flexibility of production structures, of placing the most qualified staff, workers and technicians at the disposal of the educative system, in order to evaluate the evolution of the production process and its educative needs.

The decline of education
Some major mutations have taken place in the field of labour and of non-formal education. Production structures which do not change, are indeed destined for rapid disappearance. Formal education has the possibility of continuing without mutation, but at the cost of progressive marginalisation. The resurgence of education will occur - in the same way as that of productivity - through a stimulation of

research and of cultural action. As far as education is concerned, an equilibrium between cognitive knowledge ('savoir'), action knowledge ('savoir-faire') and existential knowledge ('savoir-être') may stimulate a positive dynamic in the face of the existing educative inertia.

"Apathy and resignation among young people usually reflect a lack of self-confidence, stemming from repeated school failures and labour market" (JALLADE, 1985). The origin of these failures is often the lack of creative activities and authentic research inside the educational and production structures. The young people want results after long years of training in the educational system, or definite more or less stable periods in the productive structures.

Non-formal education is able to understand which educational questions formal educational structures fail to answer, out of which the crisis of those structures become obvious. Educational decline often goes hand in hand with industrial decline, but people talk about the latter and forget the former in relation to the force of inertia of the educational apparatus.

Stating the problem of educational decline will allow an educational renewal of the public structures, and thus a lesser appeal to the private market of education as well as to the import of external training - from professors to experts, from television programmes to instructional technology. Just as industrial decline means increased dependence for certain countries, educational decline has the same effect, not only in educational matters, but also in the field of productive activity.

The educational and productive experiences are determined by social relationships, technological development and the nature of international political and economic relations. The local educational and economic actors are faced with a world of education and labour in which the possibilities of intervention are more and more reduced. Workers, executives, teachers do participate in educational and productive activities, but they have the impression of lacking the instruments needed to modify them, according to the specific requirements of the local context. That is why local economic and educational crises are so difficult to solve, even if its actors are willing to react against them. The great scientific and technological projects are often situated outside the everyday experience of the people. One appeals to public opinion in order to get financial support for these projects, without allowing the whole of the population to see the relationships between the future of these projects and their own.

Unfortunately, educational institutions are rather poor, in scientific and technological research on the one hand, and in cultural contents, linked to a living but often disrupted culture on the other hand. On the contrary, the educational experience should concentrate on scientific and cultural development, which would permit this experience to participate in the transformations taking place in our societies.

An analysis of results rather than of educational reforms or projects demonstrates the weak points in educational policy and practice. Concerning the relation between education and the world of labour, one often notices that young people with limited schooling have difficulties, not only in integrating themselves into the productive structures, but even inside these experiments which associate education with work. The analysis of ongoing experiments - alternation, internship, professional training - reveal to us that the dualism of the labour market is not all limited by educational actions. On the contrary, it is even intensified because the non-formal educational actions, which are richer in content, are very selective by nature.

The relation or non-relation with the productive structure is very important in the education of the young, especially in an era of rapid technological mutation.

> Certainly, it is technological progress that modifies the qualification structure and demands an effort of professional training, but it is the labour market's own dynamic, and the confrontation between economic and social constraints which prevent the implementation of this professional training of the young at the desired site, namely inside the factories themselves. Such a phenomenon reinforces the destructive aspects of technological progress (LARUE DE TOURNEMINE, 1983, p. 256).

Reinforcement of technical and scientific competences on the one hand, and strong cultural development by creating and utilising cultural goods on the other hand : this is not a contradictory approach. It may well be the solution to survival from inside a society facing major transformations of its productive structures.

Transformations of the world of labour and new technologies : transfers of technologies and transfers of training

But without understanding the driving forces behind the introduction of new technologies, and particularly their interaction with changing patterns of international division of labour, it is hard to achieve effective social control over choice of technology, and to assure that machines will fit the need of the people rather than the other way round (ERNST, 1983, p. 227).

Research is necessary to see the implications on employment concerning the introduction of new technologies, changes in the functions of work, specialisation and possibilities of controlling production and the production process (BJORN-ANDERSEN et al., 1984). Transfers of technology and training are often looked at in economic terms, but the most interesting analysis consists of evaluating the impact of those transfers on the reinforcement of local and national production capacities. This evaluation could help to avoid metaphysical discussions on the meaning of these transfers.

Educational transfers in our societies go hand in hand with scientific and technological ones and in the context of dominant economic models, even if these transfers, as far as formal educational structures are concerned, are often delayed in time. Part of the dominant social classes and of bureaucracy, who control the access to economic and administrative power, often operate as a drag on the adaptability of the educational system. The internationalisation of the economy makes these resistances even more vulnerable, because international competition provokes, to a certain degree, a crisis within inefficient productive and (though less often) administrative structures.

Concerning the new educational technologies, the big risk brought along by introducing pedagogical informatics - and tomorrow, pedagogical robotics - is the risk of ultimately reinforcing the educational dualism between social groups and countries. But this dualism is not the result of those new technologies, but rather of selections, discriminations, or educational categorisations which exclude some people and advantage others. A careful democratic consideration of educational informatics and robotics will appear to be essential if one wants to use scientific discoveries in a perspective of educational and cultural democracy, and not as the ultimate means of selection and consequently of discrimination.

The transformation of the world of production, of which technological transfers are only one aspect, provokes the acceleration - and in some cases retardation - of the workers' mobility from one country to another, in different ways. On the international level, workers' mobility is estimated anywhere between 19.7 million and 21.7 million economic migrants in 1980 (BIT, 1985) and 12.6 million refugees during the same period. The 'receiving' societies tend to consider these workers as a burden. They fail to see the wealth of cultural contributions they bring with them.

The implications of the transformations of the world of labour for the states also deserve an analysis; once again, reflection is retarded. This becomes apparent when one takes a look at multinational enterprises. To a certain extent, they are already incapable of managing the structural changes they themselves have provoked.

Small, intermediate and large companies and small, intermediate and large countries undergo crises and or development in a different way. Likewise, facing industrial decline, the state apparatuses react differently.

> As far as the state apparatus is concerned, the perception of an ongoing decline requiring an intervention of any kind is determined by : (1) the emergence of particularly menacing crises because they translate in an exemplary way (2) the socio-political problems affecting large companies or entire enterprise systems, represented by (3) interest groups who are sufficiently powerful and influential to provoke the intervention of the state (PICHIERRI, 1985, p. 245).

According to the size of the company, a specific type of training is used. Small and intermediate companies find themselves, in a way, confronted with a need for polyvalent training, and in another way, with the outflow of competent employees after training on-the-job or formalised training (LUTZ, 1984).

Crisis and development of productive structures, crisis and development of public structures on the national and international level, crisis of national states have led to a situation of international crisis. The crisis we are involved in is a world-wide one. It is the result of the crisis "of mundane structures set up during the past fifteen years by the movement of multinationalisation" (MICHALAT, 1985, p. 8). Indeed, if national regulations are not adjusted to the contemporary situation any more, neither do the multinationals establish a new type of regulation at a world scale on their own, whatever judgement one may have about this type of regulation.

Why cultural action and research?

The more production and education drift apart from cultural adventure and scientific research, the larger becomes the crisis they face. An evaluation of this matter is worth carrying out. How can we fight off this alienation?

Technicity and imagination of cultural action in all its appearances, and the rigour of scientific effort in its research activities are contributions of method and of substance to the education of the young and adults and to creativity in the production process.

Culture at school : are we asking too much? Scientific research in study and production : how do we translate this evidence into educational and productive practices? Perhaps the encounter of scientists, poets, musicians, painters with those who are studying and working - and not only with the elites - is the stake of modern education and production.

Technological innovations

One of the main problems in technological innovation is the participation of the actors involved in productive activity. The so-called resistance to innovation often is just a reaction against being excluded from the decision process concerning the innovation and against marginalisation and loss of power of those who are affected by the innovation.

The speed of transformation of the world of

production demands a certain capacity of innovation and technological creation, and not simply of adaptability. Innovation and creation cannot be an occasional activity, nor can they be limited to one part of the productive structure. Innovation is not necessarily linked to a centralised management model nor to a decentralised one. It is located at all levels of the productive structure.

Innovation is often a reflection of the health of the production structures as well as of a given society. The aperture towards innovation and its translation into new forms of production and social organisation are indeed signs of a lively, moving social context, which shows curiosity and is capable of self-questioning.

Technological innovation is also a reflection of policies concerning technical and scientific development. Reductionist views of science and technology can also slow down creation and innovation. A Manichean vision that would want science and technology - and their instruments - to be able to solve everything or, would on the contrary, in the name of a false humanism, resist the contribution of new instruments offered by science and technology, would be very negative for creation and innovation. The relationship between man and machine - whatever its nature - can be very fruitful for human development. Man, machine and power : the third pole must also be taken into consideration. Power tends to measure the interest of scientific and technological development and innovation in relation to its own maintenance, and not necessarily to the benefits for society as a whole.

Could it be that sociology of science, as it has been conceived up to now, is limited? The challenge is indeed to study the consequences of scientific and technological research and development for social relations and for relations between the peoples of the world. Such a sociology would permit a better understanding of the progressive or conservative nature of resistance to research or innovation.

Not only researchers or people who are responsible for the use and the maintenance of the machine are interested in innovation. Innovation concerns all people who are active in productive and social life, but, unfortunately, this interest does not necessarily mean that the entire population gets a benefit from innovation... There are also the 'dead' and the 'wounded' in bankrupt businesses, there are labourers out of work, farmers in distress, through innovation processes neglecting social and economic realities. Is innovation a new tool of selection, or a generalisation of technical and scientific culture ? The answer to this question is worth being studied in different productive and social structures.

Innovation is not only found in the area of technology and science. Social and aesthetic innovations are important as well, although they often meet more resistance on their way than technological and scientific ones.

Transfers of technology may mean innovation and regression at the same time. Thus transfers that were not asked for or patents that were imposed put a brake on innovation and creativity of those countries who pay a heavy price for these transfers without getting any benefit from them. An efficient transfer is conditioned by its capacity of stimulating research and innovation, and not by substituting itself for it. Such innovative transfers have only taken place where there has been a participation of interested populations.

Innovations, like innovators, need a favourable environment. As a parallel to the innovators we find those who, for the sake of commercial, personal or ideological competition, have the function of opposing innovation. That is why innovators should not only put the problem in terms of techniques and methods of innovation, but also in strategic terms. Anyway, innovations may also take place in circumstances of material, social and technological difficulty, and maybe these innovations are the most interesting and the most resistant. One refers mainly to innovations in countries which are characterized by a diffusion of scientific and technological development. The source of innovation also gets its inspiration in more difficult circumstances.

Resistances to innovation and creativity
Innovation and originality in production are closely linked to the curious and non-conformistic mind. Hierarchical control is often restrictive and blocks either the innovation itself or its application.

Resistance to innovation is located on the structural level as well as on the level of the person who should be actively involved in the innovation process. The hierarchy tends to facilitate it as long as it can reinforce central power but on the contrary, to oppose it if power will possibly be questioned. Likewise the person who is affected by the innovation, will resist if the innovation might diminish or wipe out his power to negotiate within the productive structure. Psychological resistances may thus occur due to previous negative experiences.

Furthermore, technological innovation is often limited to certain areas of production or to islands inside the productive structure. These innovations can therefore contribute to a reduction or even provoke a negative reaction from the side of the excluded. Thus, new marginal categories vis-a-vis technological innovation are being created. These categories often consist of people with a low level of schooling - who are excluded in a quasi-permanent way from the labour market. This marginality causes difficulties in mastering a technology which, from now on, will be part of everyday life.

It becomes clear now that resistance to innovation is primarily a resistance to re-structuring which 'restructured' subjects undergo, and for whom the innovative aspect is completely disadvantageous. It is indeed not a contradiction that the same individuals who are very open to technological innovation concerning domestic, social or leisure time activities, resist innovations in their own working places. It is a little too easy to believe that a generalised attitude and readiness towards technological innovation exists, not linked to the concrete situation in which the innovation takes place.

On the economic level, countries who dispose of important interior or exterior markets to absorb their products, naturally have more important possibilities to introduce innovations and technologies in the productive process, because these innovations are immediately profitable on the economic level. Thus, the manufacturing companies can immediately take profits from their investments, and can often allow their workers to participate in these advantages.

While talking about technological innovation, one often tends to look only at limited aspects of this process. Innovations are indeed profitable if a global strategy is set up, which allows us to find answers to the contradiction between competition and cooperation. This is the case in the Japanese productive structures, where one finds a regulation for both competition and cooperation : competition between industries, namely on the national market, and cooperation on the national level, in order to face international competition.

Technological innovation in the production process is closely linked to the level of participation of workers in productive activities; the contradiction existing within societies with a free market economy as well as within those with a planned economy, is to implement technological innovations in production without accompanying them with a permanent participation in the productive process. In a participational perspective, one might think that innovation could stimulate democracy in our working places and societies. This may be true for productive structures with a high degree of innovation. It is not true for the structures that are only partially affected by technological innovation. The gap between those who participate and those who are marginal to innovation leads indeed to types of dualism which are contradictory to democratisation. This is particularly true, in certain countries, in the military field or in small groups, or even castes - removed from the rest of the population, living in islands with their own laws, their privileges and their continuity of power.

With a lot of difficulties, education and on-the-job-training are being transformed into permanent educational processes. Technological innovations nowadays are linked to several variables of an economic, social, cultural and organisational nature - and not only to technical variables. But an observation of educational practice shows that the initial and continuing education is still far away from taking into account these different variables, and that the social, cultural, and managerial contents are relatively absent in the educational activity.

The nature of technology and the dynamics of its development also deserve a careful analysis. Technological creation means training towards production, creativity and capacity of analysis.

Education can play a major role in turning innovations into instruments of selection or, on the contrary, in permitting everyone to participate in them by means of a policy of positive discrimination.

On the one hand we have an educational activity reflecting technological innovation of the production process, and on the other hand an innovation in the educational process itself. At the present day, the most urgent innovation may well be the educational one, in order to limit or overcome the decline that hits the school and university structures as well as continuing education.

Technological innovations, especially if they are not achieved by means of transfer, can cause quite serious ruptures in the everyday culture of individuals. Transforming the nature of production is a choice which can provoke serious damage, not only at the cultural, but also at the psychical level. Hence the need for developing, as far as possible, cultural policies allowing innovations to become an instrument of development, not of personal and cultural regression for those who are either touched or excluded. Concerning this matter, education can play an important role by enriching not only its technological contents, but also its cultural ones. Better relations between the technical-scientific culture and the humanist culture might prevent the division of countries, and of social and socio-professional groups, from one another, into those who have access to technological innovation and those who are excluded from it.

Technological innovation needs a favourable soil to grow on, to be applied and transferred.

In the phase of application and transfer of innovation, initial and continuing education as well as independent study can play an important role in preventing adaptation and transfers to mean alienation of individuals and cultures, a social disorder and new forms of social dualism.

Education for innovation means bringing the instructional systems, namely the professional ones now existing, into discussion. New contents and methods are to be faced, focused on the 'savoir-faire' as well as the 'savoir-être' and stimulating the divergent mind and, from the very beginning, any form of individual learning. The latter must above all, as we said before, be founded on the capacity of analysis, of production, of creation, of creativity, and needs the contribution of scientists, technicians, artists, the only ones who are capable of stimulating innovations as a permanent dimension of the educational process.

REFERENCES

Amendola, M., Heraud, J.A. and Lanzavecchia G. (1983) 'L'innovation : vers une nouvelle révolution technologique', Notes et Etudes Documentaires, Paris, n° 4727/4728

----- (1983) 'Aspects de l'automatisation - Quelles logiques économiques et sociales?', Critique de l'économie politique, n°22

Bertrand, O. (1986) Ressources humaines et compétitivité de l'économie italienne, Cereq, Paris

Bertrand, O. and Noyelle, T.J. (1985) Gestion des ressources humaines et technologie aux Etats-Unis, Cereq, Paris

Bidault, F. (1985) 'Changements techniques et mutations de l'appareil productif', Mutations technologiques et formations, n°223

Bit (1985) Le travail dans le monde

Bjorn-Andersen, N. and Traesborg, M. (1984) Work qualifications and education requirements en-route to the information society, Cedefop, Berlin

Bosworth, D. (ed.) (1983) The employment consequences of technological change, Macmillan Press, London,

Caciari, P., Erlicher L., Ferrari A., Mammucari, F., Migliore, F., Omodei Zorini E., Osimo, B., Passerini, A., Pieroni, W. and Schweizer, K. (1985) Le 150 ore e la formazione professionale in Azienda - Il caso Italtel, Franco Angeli, Milano

Capechhi, V. (1985) 'Appunti per una riflessione, sulla metodologia della ricerca sociologica, Quaderni di sociologia, n°4-5

Carcano, M., Di Francesco, G., Provasi, G. and Taronna, P. (1985) 'Automazione d'Ufficio', Quaderni di Formazione ISFOL, n° 4/85

Cerych, L. et al. (1985) La formation aux nouvelles technologies d'information et de la communication : perspectives européennes, IEEPS

Chesnais, F. (1983) 'Enjeux de la nouvelle technologie', Amérique latine, n° 13

Coriat, B. (1985) 'Technologies, emplois, salaires, dans l'industrie automobile américaine', Travail, n°9

Cortes, M. and Bocock, P. (1984) North-South technology transfer, a case study of petrochemicals in Latin America, The Johns Hopkins University Press, London

Dorf, R.C. (1983) Robotics and Automated Manufacturing, Reston Publishing Company Inc., Reston

Ernst, D. (1983) The global race in micro-electronics, Campus Verlag, Frankfurt

Fasano, C. (1985) 'Beyond Computers - Education', European Journal of Education, Vol. 20, n° 2-3

Hubbard, G. (1984) 'Social and educational effects

of technological change', British Journal of educational studies, Vol. XXXII, n° 2
Huet, M. (1985) 'La gestion de l'emploi féminin et masculin obéit-elle à des logiques différentes ?', Les temps modernes, n° 462
Jallade, J.P. (1985) 'Youth unemployment and education' in T. Husen et al., The International Encyclopedia of Education, Pergamon, Oxford
Kaplinsky, R. (1984) Automation, the technology and society, Longman, London
Kochan, T.A. (1985) Challenges and Choices facing American Labor, MIT Press, Cambridge
Larue De Tournemine, R. (1983) L'innovation vers une nouvelle révolution technique, La documentation française, Paris
Larricia, G. (1984) 'Il calcolatore nell'educazione : dall' approccio tecnologico a quello epistemologico', I problemi di Ulisse, Vol. XVI, Sasc. XCVI
----- (1983) 'L'avenir de la technologie japonaise', Cahiers du Japon, numéro spécial
Lipietz, A. (1986) 'La seconde grande crise du XXème siècle' in Gemdev, Economie mondiale, économies nationales et multinationales, Cahier n°5
Lipietz, A. (1985) Miracles et mirages, Paris
Lutz, B. (1984) Problemi della formazione professionale nella piccola e media impresa, Cedefop, Berlin
----- (1983) Méthodes utilisées aux USA dans le domaine de la planification et du développement des technologies, Ministère de la Recherche et de l'Industrie, Centre de prospective et d'évaluation, Paris, Etude n° 12
Michalet, L.A. (1985) 'Les multinationales sont-elles innovatrices dans les technologies de pointe', Multinational Info
Penn, R. and Scattergood, H. 'Deskilling or enskilling? : an empirical investigation of recent theories of the labour process', The British Journal of Sociology, Vol. XXXVI, n°4
Pichierri, A. (1985) 'Le déclin industriel : une étude critique et sélective de la littérature anglo-américaine', Informations sur les sciences sociales, n°2
Pim, D. (1985) 'Technology as the illusion of order', Futures, n° 4
Ruffier, J., Bunel J., Supervielle, M. and Walter, J. (1985) L'automatisation réussie dans les PMI à faibles ressources (Argentine et Uruguay), Groupe Lyonnais de Sociologie indus-

trielle, Bron
Sandkull, B. (1983) 'Using new technology to prevent economic and industrial democracy', Paper prepared for the International Conference on Future Prospects for Industrial and Economic Democracy at Dubrovnik, Mimeo, Yugoslavia
Stoneman, P. (1983) <u>The Economic analysis of technological change</u>, Oxford University Press, New York
----- (1984) 'The impact of information technology on employment, working conditions and industrial relations', <u>Work Labour Report</u>, ILO, chapter 7
Tucker, J. (ed.) (1984) <u>Education, training and the new technologies</u>, A report of the Scottish Council for Educational Technology Conference 'Look Out for Learners' (16-17 March 1983), Kogan Page, Nichols Publishing Company, London, New York
Various Authors (1986) <u>Technological change</u>, Commonwealth Secretariat, London
Vinokur, A. (1984) 'A propos de la mesure des dépenses publiques d'éducation', <u>Revue française de finances publiques</u>, n° 6
Weber, J. (1985) <u>Tomorrow's world, Computers</u>, Arco Publishing, New York
Winterton, J. (1984) 'Industrial Democracy and New Technology', <u>The industrial tutor</u>, vol. 3, n° 10

Chapter Four
PERSPECTIVE OF AN ENVIRONMENTAL ORIENTED ECONOMY

Theo POTMA
Centre for Energy Conservation
Delft, The Netherlands

Introduction
This paper treats primarily the second part of the conference-title: "Adult education and the challenges of the 1990s". What are the challenges of the near future? What are the promises, what are the threats? How do we have to respond to threats of nuclear war, massive unemployment and lack of food for so many people? Questions which are very important for our youth. The opening paper by Walter Leirman speaks of "the optimistic sixties and the crisis-laden eighties"; "economic and cultural shockwaves leading to changes in themes, methods and policies"; "a radical and worldwide crisis"; "a new scientific paradigm which we call social-communicative".

In my opinion the sixties were too optimistic about the technical and economic possibilities on our globe, the seventies were too optimistic about the possibilities to adapt our society to a changing reality and the eighties are too pessimistic about both. What we need is a realistic approach to the "hard-ware" possibilities on our globe and the "soft-ware" possibilities to change our social behaviour. As an environmentalist I must say that in my opinion our problems are not primarily caused by the limitations of our global environment. Our problem is our incapability to adapt our social-economic behaviour to the changing conditions. The generation that is pulling the strings, has a lot of brain, a lot of institutions, a lot of computer systems, a lot of information and a lot of power but too little imagination and too little idealism.

So we must hope that the new generation, our youth, which shows already a remarkable sense of realism, will be able to change our social behaviour and to grasp the existing perspective.

In the following paragraphs I will limit my contribution to the socio-economic perspective which seems positive and promising but inevitably needs a clear change in our socio-economic priorities.

Environment and welfare
Inhabitants of every country want their government to establish an economic policy which will lead to a high state of welfare. Welfare can be defined as the satisfaction of wants evoked by dealing with scarce means. Satisfaction of wants, of course, is an aspect of one's personal experience. The level of welfare of society as a whole is influenced by a number of factors which are strongly interrelated. The seven most important are according to Hueting (HUETING, 1984) :

1. the package of produced goods and services;
2. the scarce environmental goods in the broad sense, inclusive of space, energy, natural resources, plants and animal species;
3. time or leisure time;
4. the distribution of scarce goods or the income-distribution;
5. the working condition;
6. employment;
7. the safety of our future as far as this depends on our dealing with scarce goods.

Every economic policy aiming at a higher level of welfare has to do with all these seven interdependent factors. Every economic policy therefore reflects a certain priority value for each factor. An environmental economic policy gives a very high priority to saving the environment which means saving and maintaining the possibilities of our local and global environment to contribute to our welfare in a direct way and also (via our production system) in an indirect way. As a contrast to this, the economic policy of our time continues to give top priority to the increase in the volume of produced goods. This policy which aims primarily at a higher production of goods seems and is said to be profitable for the consumer. In the past, and probably in the short run this may be true. In the long run, however, the consumer is probably better off with an environmental policy, due to the fact that neglecting the environment increases the risk of overshoots. This means that the exploitation level of the environment for the benefit of more production and consumption is so high that a state of continuity is disturbed. As a result, an ever greater part of our productive efforts has to be applied to repair the indispensable functions of our surroundings. So, small profits in the short run could lead to great losses in the long run.

Environment and economy
What is happening on the "hard-ware-side" of our economy can be illustrated by Figures 4.1 to 4.3. Figure 4.1 shows the situation of production and consumption in an infinite environment (M). The environment being the supplier of the basic materials extracted from the soil (steel, copper, aluminium, etc.) but also the supplier of natural materials (food, fish, wood, cotton, etc.), fuel (oil, gas, coal) and environmental functions (supply of fresh water, sunlight, clean air, space, etc.) but also of the so-called "life support functions" (cleaning of air, water and soil, regulation of oxygen and carbon dioxyde level, generation of genes and special material useful for medicines, etc.). Figure 4.2 illustrates the increasing production of the decreasing environment. The production, especially the heavy capital-intensive production, mainly transforms the input supplied by the environment. Increasing production means in this situation an increasing use of environment. As a result the environmental scarcity starts to develop. It gets more difficult to extract the required fuels, raw materials from the environment and the environmental functions (space, clean air, fresh water, etc.) are more difficult to maintain. Later on (Figure 4.3) extra installations (B), labour and capital are required to extract the same supply for production and consumption from the environment and to treat the polluting emissions (Z). The amount of labour and capital available for direct net production of goods will therefore _relatively_ diminish.

Perspective of an Environmental Oriented Economy

Figure 4.1

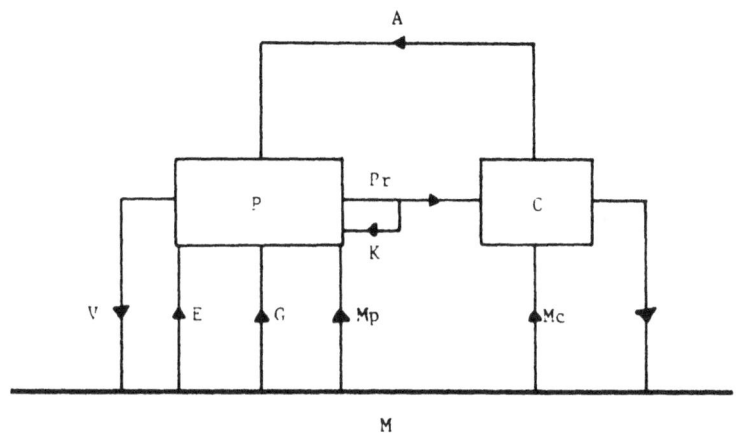

C : Consumption
V : Polluting emission
P : Production
E : Fuel-imput
C : Raw material input
M_p : Environmental production functions
     (water, space, clean air, sunlight)
M_c : Environmental consumer functions
PR : Production goods
K : Capital return
A : Labour

Figure 4.2

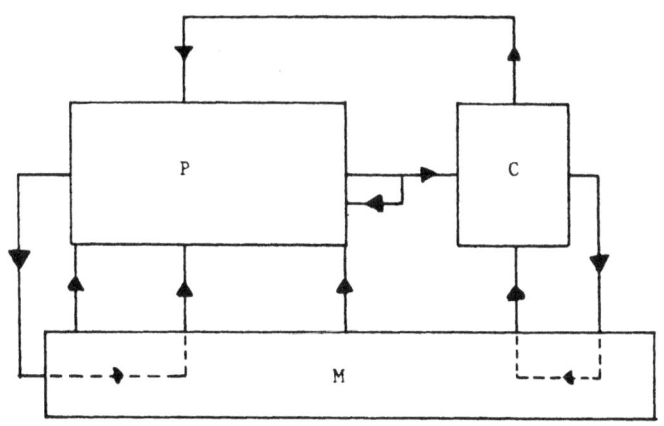

Perspective of an Environmental Oriented Economy

Figure 4.3

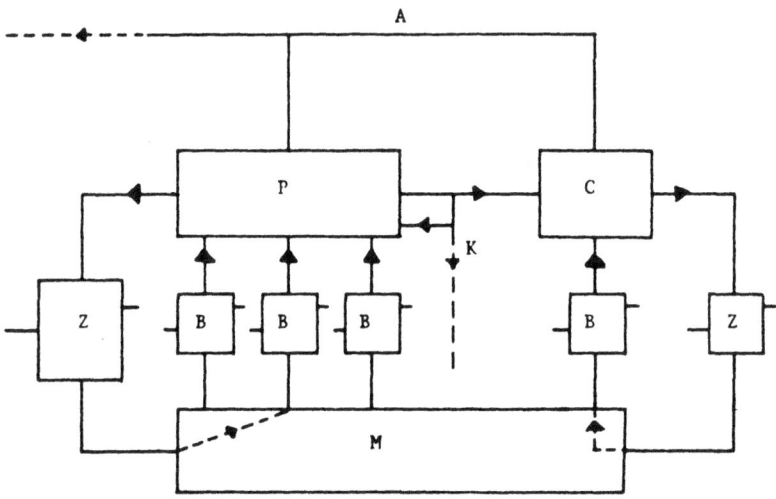

B : Extra activities to extract the required supply (drilling isle, recycling installations, water purification)
Z : Installation for waste treatement and emission reduction.

A dominant question here is whether technical inventions are able to change our production sufficiently in such a way that production increase can nevertheless be combined with a simultaneous improvement of the environment. Personally and as a technician, I am of the opinion that technical innovations alone are not sufficient. Mainly because of the growing world population, the already existing environmental overshoots and the unequal distribution of "production-welfare" over the world, the rich countries are no longer in a position to claim automatically a higher income (a higher "production-welfare"). In discussions about the required environmental measures, however, this message is often regarded as too "pessimistic" and therefore rejected. At this point - in my opinion - ideas about a sustainable economy, ideas about an environmental economy and ideas about Christian responsibility and "stewardship" should lead to firm statements and practical measures aim-

Perspective of an Environmental Oriented Economy

ing at the saving of our environmental treasures and to safeguard our future. Such measures are generally regarded as a threat to our income, welfare and employment rate. This is a very unrealistic and pessimistic view. Welfare and employment can profit strongly by the environmental economic priority and the consumer income is safeguarded for the future. The only drawback is a possible reduction in consumer income in the short run.

This foreseen possible short term sacrifice in consumer income is however by no means dramatic. The main reason is that in the (over?) developed countries, further increase of production usually goes hand in hand with a simultaneous decrease in other welfare factors (factor 2, 7, 3 and 5). So, the net contribution of consumer income to welfare is diminishing. Far more important seems the safeguarding of the production potential itself as this will probably decrease if the environmental potential is drained.

A national discussion

Which types of measures are required to realize a shift to an environmental economy? Which positive and negative effects on the short and long run are to be expected if our economic priorities are changed? This question was a main target in the "CE-scenario-study" (POTMA, 1982), which formed a part of the "national discussion on energy" in The Netherlands. The CE-scenario was a unique experiment because:

1. the scenario-study was an instrument in a national discussion about the consequences of various social-economic policies;
2. the Dutch governement was to a high degree a formal partner in this discussion;
3. the study was an integral and open scientific confrontation between two economic policies;
4. the study was subject to an extensive preparation and accompaninment by (three) official committees during the full study period 1979-82 (AER, 1978).

Perspective of an Environmental Oriented Economy

The CE-scenario
The CE-scenario can only be evaluated by comparing it with the projections made by the Ministry of Economic Affairs (EZ) and the Central Planning Office based on government policy. These projections will be referred to hereafter as the EZ Reference Scenario (AER, 1980) which reflects the traditional economic priorities. On various points concerning energy and environment the CE-scenario suggests measures and developments different from those in the EZ Reference Scenario. These points of difference are:

1. Energy management
   Additional energy-saving and use of renewable energy sources, application of combined heat and power generation in electricity production (in addition to limited use of coal).
2. Environmental protection
   Further measures to improve the quality of the air, water and soil and reduce the amount of waste products (recycling).
3. Agriculture
   Agricultural policy includes reducing the use of artificial fertilizer and pesticides; transporting surpluses of manure to areas with shortage of manure; reduction of the manipulations with ground water level; reduction of the number of reallotments of holdings and a change in the nature of these; mechanization, but with smaller and lighter machines; more crop rotation; less canalization of brooks; restoration and maintenance of hedges and the like.
4. Traffic and transport
   Greater emphasis on public transport and slow traffic rather than the use of private cars.
5. Inner city renewal
   Improvement of inner cities, further renewal and renovation schemes.
6. Extended durability
   Extending the useful life of durable consumer goods.
7. Economic structure
   Encouragement of the service sector, partly because services like repair firms and corner shops fit into an environmental programme, partly so as to reduce expansion of

Perspective of an Environmental Oriented Economy

environmentally unacceptable activities under pressure of the high unemployment.

8. Distribution of work
Shortening of the number of working hours per week and per worker together with an extension of the daily working hours of factories.

Comparability
Considerable attention was paid to the comparability base of the two main scenarios during preparation of the CE-scenario. An official body was appointed by the Dutch Government to ensure adequate comparability of the respective scenarios, particularly with an eye to their employment in the 'broad public debate' on energy policy in the Netherlands. There was also an intense consultation and co-operation with "official" Dutch institutions.

The result of these joint consultations was that the architects of the two scenarios, viz. the Centre for Energy Conservation on the one hand and the Ministry of Economic Affairs on the other, based their work on:

1. the same basic macro-economic data (world trade development, balance of payments, financial deficit, etc.);
2. the environmental figures, costs, and reducing effects per measure agreed upon with the Central Bureau of Statistics;
3. the same fuel price developments for oil, coal and gas;
4. the same relative investments costs for all measures used to save energy, as well as for renewable energy resources;
5. the same method for calculating the final total fuel consumption level in the year 2000. The CE calculations are based (as far as possible and as far as is known) on the methods used in the governmental Central Planning Office's energy model.

Agreement was not reached on the cost of electricity generated in nuclear reactors. The CE bases its calculations on the parity principle, i.e. a market equilibrium is assumed for electricity produced from coal, oil, gas or uranium, assuming 'clean' production methods. Up till now the Ministry

Perspective of an Environmental Oriented Economy

of Economic Affairs has employed a rather low price for nuclear-based electricity.

The economic effects of the CE-scenario were calculated by the Foundation for Economic Studies in Amsterdam. Calculations on the ministry's reference scenario were performed on the basis of the Central Planning Office's economic model.

Although different economic models have been used, intensive negotiations were held to guarantee the comparability of the respective results. Discovered discrepancies have led to adjustments to such a degree that one can, under the circumstances, fairly speak of maximum feasible comparability.

Table 4.1

Perspective of an Environmental Oriented Economy

Results

	CE	EZ
Macro-economic growth 1980-2000	+ 28%	+ 28%
Consumption per head 1980-2000	+ 4%	+ 7%
Fuel consumption 1980-2000	- 25%	+ 10%
Electricity use 1980-2000	+ 6%	+ 38%
Unemployment in 2000	200 000	635 000
Working hours per week in 2000	- 29%	- 25%
SO_2 emission in 2000	119,000 tons	467,000 tons
NO_x emission in 2000	338,000 tons	517,000 tons
Livability in cities and landscape quality	improved	deteriorated

Measures and policy instruments
The proposed measures mean in essence <u>internationalization of the costs of the losses of environmental functions</u> caused or expected in the future. The instruments used for this are price manipulation and direct measures. The effects on the pattern of production and consumption have been estimated with the aid of calculated or estimated elasticities.

The greatest possible use has been made of the following set of instruments. The costs of the measures are defrayed by <u>charges levied on products (on the domestic market) of polluting activities</u> from both home and abroad. The products therefore undergo a real price increase. For the sake of the employment effect wages are not compensated for this. In the model the desired effect occurs endogenously because the real wages do not rise more rapidly than productivity. In these conditions impairment of the competitive position is obviated on both the domestic market (by products from abroad) and foreign markets. Together with the adjustment of the wage rate, this forms a sufficient guarantee to render permanent the positive effect of environmental measures and employment. The method at the same time prevents the flight of polluting activities abroad, for instance to developing countries.

For an industrialized country as wealthy as the Netherlands, the scenario regards full employment as a primary objective, second only to a safe environment. Self-support, in the sense of earning one's own bread and butter, is part of life's essence. Loss of potential in this respect will in all probability lead to a loss of welfare. Wide scale unemployment is moreover a destabilizing factor in society.

At present, the greatest obstacle standing in the way of a sound environmental policy is probably the belief that conservation can be achieved only at the expense of employment. However, such a proposition ignores the truism that the environment and energy are scarce goods; to obtain or preserve them, production factors have to be employed. In the industrialized countries, 80 to 95% of national income goes to the factor labour. A given level of production and consumption requires more labour when accomplished in conjunction with environmental conservation than without. This labour is however employed for non-market goods. And since wages are no more than a claim to produced goods, environmental measures amount to a relative reduction of the wage rate - or its growth - for a given package of goods and services produced by the government. It is not employment that is in conflicting interest with the environment, but rather production (plus consumption), whereby expenditure on waste treatment and the like is regarded as a cost item, as it should be.

On the strength of this reasoning, wages have, in the econometric model in which the scenario has been worked out, been simultaneously reduced in proportion to the estimated costs of the measures taken. Insofar as environmental measures are the

Perspective of an Environmental Oriented Economy

cause of business bankruptcies now occurring, this is due to a failure to draw logical conclusions with respect to the wage rate and put them into practice. The relative effect of the measures on unemployment is illustrated in Figure 4.4.

Figure 4.4

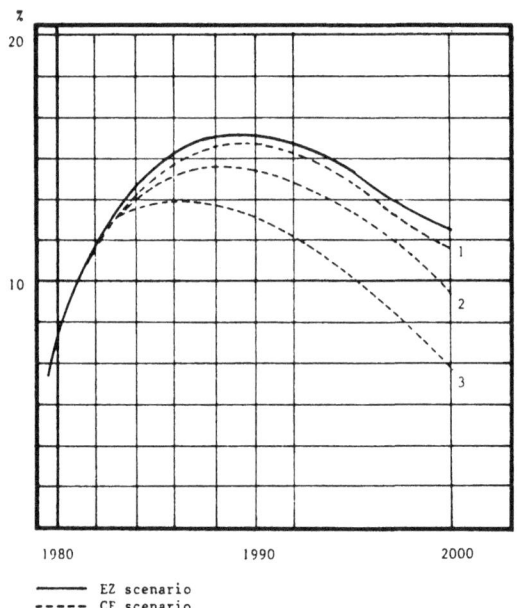

Unemployment percentages:
1. energy policy
2. environmental policy
3. changes in consumption pattern caused by lower taxes for the service sector

The government subsidies to encourage energy-saving and the development of forms of energy derived from the sun are financed by an extra increase in the price of energy and the introduction of progressive rates of charges. (Such measures could best be introduced in a period of temporarily falling world market prices as is now happening with the oil prices). The lag in the increase of productivity in agriculture as a result of the environmental measures leads to relative price increases for agricultural products; remuneration of the farmer's work undergoes no relative fall. In transport policy the point of departure is making the fixed costs of the private car as variable as possible. In addition serious parking charges are introduced and no new parking garages and roads are built. As a result of the insulation and the renovation policy, rents rise. An expansion of the service sector comes about through a reduction of the VAT rate for the labour intensive services involved that fit into an environmental policy (repair and the like) or impose little of a burden on the environment, and an increased rate for the capital-intensive firms that greatly burden the environment. This too amounts to internationalization of environmental costs that are spread out over society in such a way that certain groups do not make more sacrifices than others, on the assumption of not too great interpersonal differences in the consumption package. The most important instruments used are listed below.

Instruments for an environmental oriented policy

1. higher VAT rates on environmental intensive materials and material intensive products;
2. lower VAT rates on labour intensive (environment - material - extensive) activities especially for the service and repair sector;
3. variable costs of motorcars increased (as a first step road tax via petrol price);
4. progressive fuel rates and energy tax, charges on environment intensive and polluting materials and emissions;
5. higher inland food prices, subsidies for environment-saving types of farming, financial measures to restrict agricultural production quantities per surface-area;
6. decentralization of the electricity production, reorganization of the electricity sector;
7. shorter working week, more factory hours;
8. severe environmental regulations;
9. more subsidies for environmental and energy or material saving measures.

Perspective of an Environmental Oriented Economy

Discussion
Comparison of the results shows that an environmental oriented economy will lead to a relatively lower income for the consumer. The effect is, however, very small (4% instead of 7% over a period of 20 years). All other effects are positive. The sacrifice in income is strongly compensated for by the positive effects.
This rather attractive overall result of the CE-scenario is to a great extent due to the higher employment rate compared to the reference scenario. In the CE-scenario a lot of work is created by the environmental oriented measures. The direct expenses of these measures seem to be high but the resulting "all-in costs" are rather low because of the strongly reduced unemployment costs.

It has to be taken into account that the scenario results are not absolute but only relative figures. A lower increase in world trade, a strong price increase of imported raw materials (as a result of efforts to help the developing countries), an increased scarcity of capital (as a result of efforts to generate a strong capital transfer to the developing countries) would result in a lower income. To compensate such a drop in income the number of working hours could be increased again by means of a further shift in the consumption pattern. Such a further shift, however, will this time not result in reduced costs for unemployment. Therefore the income effect would certainly be positive, but also rather low.

On the other hand an assumed possibility to increase productivity by technical innovations which at the same time reduce the environmental pressure would result in a higher income and a better environment. This is what we should try to achieve, but what we should not promise or assume because if such an assumption shows itself to be wrong, the result is disappointment, a delay in the introduction of the required measures and (again) a further deteriorated environment.

Effects of a strongly environmental oriented social economic policy
For the purpose of discussion and comparison a rough estimation of the expected short and long term effects of an environmental oriented economy are indicated in Table 2 (see next page). These estimates show the dominating long term advantages but also

Perspective of an Environmental Oriented Economy

the short term disadvantages which make such economic priorities difficult to realize.

Table 4.2

	short term	long term
- innovations, new industries	+	+
- employment	++	+
- consumers' income	-	+?
- production growth	-?	+?
- future outlook environmental intensive industries	-	-
- international dependence	+?	+
- military strength	-	-?
- military invulnerability	+?	+

REFERENCES

----- (1980) Advice AER on energy scenarios, The Hague

----- (1978) Advice of the general Dutch council on energy (AER) on the national discussion, The Hague

Drieshuis, W. a.o. (1983) Economie, energie en milieu in Nederland 1980-2000, Stichting voor Economisch Onderzoek, University of Amsterdam

Hueting, R. (1984) Results of an economic scenario that gives top priority to saving the environment instead of encouraging production growth, OECD paper

----- (1981) Ongewijzigd beleid scenario (Het Referentie Scenario), Ministerie van economische zaken, Den Haag

Potma, T. et al. (1982) Het CE-scenario, een realistisch alternatief, Centrum voor energiebesparing, Delft

Chapter Five
ECOLOGICAL EDUCATION   A FAILING PRACTICE?
OR: IS THE ECOLOGICAL MOVEMENT AN EDUCATIONAL MOVEMENT?

Marianne GRONEMEYER
Ruhr University Bochum
Federal Republic of Germany

If anybody had ever suddenly asked me "What was your first reaction to the news of April 29, 1986 - that the super-explosion, the possibility of which had hitherto been excluded by hordes of expressive and self-confident experts, had happened in the Chernobyl reactor?", then I would have answered this : "I am shaken to the bone, a laming consternation has befallen me".
   However, for reasons of both judiciousness and precision of memory - and whoever wants to counteract organized oblivion has to rely on this - I have to correct this answer. I would notably have to refrain myself and to admit that my real reaction was far less unequivocal and less adequate. It consisted much more of a contradictory mixture of feelings, to which all kinds of speculations were added. When I carefully walk down the tracks of memory and unearth the archeology of emotions, I clearly find that consternation and fear played only a minor and remote part in the irritation and commotion of the first moment. They were present as an expression of <u>consciousness</u>, which is the only adequate form of <u>understanding</u>. They were accepted in the form of the following <u>reflection</u> : only consternation, i.e. the "will to be threatened" can conjure up the will to affront reality.
   As a matter of fact, only consternation can halt our increasing loss of contact with reality. Nowadays, one cannot participate in reality for a lesser price. In the case of Chernobyl however, our sense of fear was constrained by reflection, even before it could enter into operation : "Reflection ... stays aloof from the real problem" says Peter Sloterdijk, it performs the function of "making bearable the unbearable" and of "reducing pain

to a sustainable format, which can be treated within the framework of a painless colloquial arrangement" (RÖTZER, 1986).

What was given free flow however, without any reflexive constraints, was the "catastrophile itching" (SLOTERDIJK, 1986), a "furtive pleasure" found in the catastrophe as it had happened. Acknowledgements of such "furtive pleasure" have a long-standing but deplorable tradition in our Federal Republic - witness the Mescalero affair - but our theme of ecopedagogy requires a fair account of the "furtive pleasure" side of our reaction to the catastrophe - since part of its roots lie there.

Taking pleasure in a catastrophe stems from two different impulses which are rather suspect and therefore will avoid showing their naked and true face.

The first impulse can be called relief, the soothing sense of having escaped, the magic power of survival. An objectionable, yet almost charming form of this impulse is seen in the popular prayer to saint Florian, who is invoked to restrict his kindling work to the neighbour's house and not to set fire to the owner's - if he cannot abstain from pyromania at all.

Elias Canetti has denounced this intoxication of survival as a dangerous and wicked impulse : "The situation of surviving somebody else is the central instance of proving one's power" (CANETTI, 1981, p. 27). The living person, to whom everything is still possible, is never more conscious of his vitality than in the face of a dead person whom he has survived. For a short while, an escape from mortality seems to be possible, and the survivor feels absolutely sure about his life, which is otherwise often threatened and uncertain indeed. To be sure about one's life - that is the central issue of power. "The happy feeling of actual survival is a matter of intensive lust. Once it has been admitted and legitimated, it will long for being repeated and will rapidly become an insatiable passion" (CANETTI, 1981, p. 31). But let us beware : "To show part of the pleasure evoked by the confrontation with the dead or demised person is very contrary to the established moral code" (CANETTI, 1981, p. 27).

The question now arises whether the present diagnosis reveals an anthropological or at least a socio-cultural inability of compassion or - to apply an overused pedagogical term - of involvement ? This question is all the more justified due to the fact that piety shown in the face of death fulfils only there the role of an artifact and of a cover-up for the sense of victorious survival.

For anywhere else in everyday life, survival and superiority are not suspect at all. On the contrary, it is the omnivalid criterion of success in our society and not only in the passive sense of being saved from a catastrophe, but in the active sense of serving a blow to others. Generally speaking, prestige, authority, power and success are calculated in terms of units of damage done to others in quantities of victories over others or numbers of losers left behind. The zero-sum game of Win and Loose constitutes the universal iron moral law of modern society - so much so that it has received the status of a fundamental drive : the drive towards self-preservation or affirmation of the self (BAUDRILLARD, 1982, p. 284). The official moral code superimposed on that drive then serves as a dam against proliferation and against the eruption of self-destructive tendencies. That moral has also been imposed on the educational system and its several parts.

Precisely the fact that there is no correlation between prestige and authority on the one hand and utility to the human community on the other creates the necessity of an educational system. A person cannot grow up under the fundamental contradiction between success system and officially established morality - he or she has to be educated towards its acceptance. Education fills the gap of the lacking of plausibility of our social existence. Education therefore basically supports a power structure which brings damage to the community. Therein consists the first and deepest dilemma of education, from which it cannot escape through whatever kind of inner reform.

The second impulse which tries to give a real meaning to catastrophic events is the belief that man gains wisdom from disaster. Although refuted a hundred times by history, this kind of learning theory still stands unshaken. With regard to natural disasters overwhelming man in archaic times, the association of damage and wisdom has only a reported validity - in the sense of a deduction of solemn warnings like : be conscious of the insignificance of human power, meditate on humility and modesty, abstain from Promethean assaults on heaven ...

With man-made disasters, the connection of damage and wisdom seems to be self-evident, especially when one disaster appears to announce a still bigger calamity. Thus, a few days after the news from Chernobyl broke through, people were using the unhappy term of "Threat-Catastrophe" ("Droh-Katastrophe"). It was just as if what had happened, was not a real but an "As-if-catastrophe", a theatrically mounted spectacle, a calamity-indosage, with a sufficient degree of harshness to shake the habitual indifference and the blunt consciousness of people. The catastrophe became educative, got to be seen as good. It took a meaning and hopes became attached to it. Attention was diverted from the real victims of the real catastrophe to the potential victims of future calamities who are self-oblivious humans, seized by illusions of safety and in need of liberation. They are the third party to be educated, for whose guilelessness one had finally found a weapon: disturbingly hard facts.

And mark: the statement "Something better than Chernobyl could not happen to us" did not come from the cynic leaders of the power centres, who tried to hush up the whole affair and joined in with the general frenzy of survival. The holders of that opinion were rather to be found among those tenacious but largely unsuccessful activists who tried to counteract the unimaginably destructive industrial build-up, and who sometimes suffered great personal losses. Blaming them with cynicism is, therefore, no easy matter. The afore cited statement means nothing else but this: The Chernobyl catastrophe had to happen in order to prevent the worst, namely a total Apocalypse. In a letter to the author, a German novelist formulated this message with a frightening consistency :"History is leading to death-from-frost. The surprising fact seems to be that psychic death is happening so long before physical frosty death, i.e. as a consequence of the glacial lakes which have invaded the human soul ... I'm afraid we are irreversibly drifting towards the Inferno, and if we are to save anything, then maybe only through a partial Inferno, whereby the rest of the world would stop and think. Given the rules of the game, a sacrifice of hecatombs of people looks unavoidable, and to bark against it is like barking against the moon...".

Chernobyl: a partial Inferno, an eye-opener to the mind, finally a pressing argument? <u>How much of catastrophe does man need?</u>
Our theme deals with nothing else but this

problem. Both questions raised in our title are to be situated within this dimension.

The task imposed upon me by our theme is to try to determine the relationship between environmental <u>education</u> or eco<u>pedagogy</u> and environmental <u>movement</u>. This is not a new issue, and it has been dealt with for a good number of years now. There have been quite some variations - but the general trend seems to be that ecopedagogy has shown an increasing respect and a growing modesty towards the social-ecological movement.

At the beginning of the 70s, we registered pedagogical macro-phantasies concerning the question of how to raise an overdue consciousness of the ecological crisis within broad layers of the population. By the end of the 70s, at the time when a relatively broad ecological movement had come into existence - admittedly without much support from the pedagogical professions - the question was raised in which way institutionalized education could realize a complement to that movement. However, since the beginning of the 80s, the question is how adult education can itself learn from the new social movements : by then, it had become clear that those movements were also educative movements.

Yet, if we put the question in this general form, we do not touch the core of our theme. There is solid ground for the <u>presumption</u> that the proper definitions of environmental education and environmental <u>movement</u> have been curiously blurred. Both even seem to have exchanged their proprium or formal object. When we take the concepts in their logical sense, environmental education indicates or delineates a <u>learning field</u> whereas the environmental movement establishes an <u>action field</u>. In actual fact, however, ecopedagogy is interested primarily in the politically acting subject, whereas the ecological movement is interested in the learning subject. Both therefore are taking the wrong course, and fail in realizing environmental action as well as environmental learning. Quid est demonstrandum (to be proved).

First of all, we should ask ourselves : How can we justify the thesis that ecopedagogy is not directed primarily at ecological learning, but at concrete political practice? Are the actual facts not contradicting this thesis almost to the detail ? Do we not complain about the fact that a brief phase of political-educational theory building - where the interdependence of political action and political learning was not only accepted as a given fact but also demanded as a basic principle of programming (GIESECKE, 1972) - has been followed by a phase in which at least institutionalized political education is getting radically separated from any political practice to such a degree that institutions of political education have become learning spaces freed of all politics? This is what we find, and for the financial support of political education the authorities use this separation as a decisive criterion of selection.

When I say that environmental education is practice-oriented, then I mean that the learning process, which it organizes, initiates and guides, is turned into instrumental action. It incorporates this as a goal outside of itself. The proper intention, therefore, is not learning itself, but a specific and determinable change of political everyday options as a result of learning. And several specific changes then should culminate into a global societal change. Revolutionary impatience has taken the place of the patience of the small steps and the forbearance which learning so often requires. But the basic interest is with the result of the process and with the predetermined objective, and not with the process itself and its meandering paths. Ecopedagogy is "persuasion labour", and not the staging of learning stories with an open end. It does not aim at surprise and multiplicity, but at a consensus of opinion as a basis for common political action. Ecopedagogy wants to stage the victorious march of the better arguments - which, according to Habermas, "exert a curiously uncoercive coercion"(HABERMAS, 1971, p. 137), it strives at common agreement, it wants to replace the "false" with the "true" consensus.

To me, a further insoluble dilemma of ecopedagogy is its intention to realize, or better, to produce ecological consciousness and environmental practice. The production of ecological consciousness and ecological action requires a high price : the abandonment of ecological learning. When talking about failing practice, I do mean more than the fact that organized ecological learning misses the connection with a concomitant practice - and therefore ought to refine its instruments.

It is rather like this : ecological conscience and ecological conduct (HELLER, 1978) are basically incompatible with the modality of production in whatever form, even the pedagogical one. I hereby use the concept of life conduct, because the concept of "practice" is embedded in a tradition of progress, perfection and the duty to always do better - which is contradictory to ecology. The realization of a dynamic balance between living, thinking, learning and acting through an uninterrupted interplay cannot be guaranteed by means of a procedure which solely aims at giving the consumer a finished product, and which is only engaged in for the sake of that product. One may doubt whether intentional and goal-directed educative action can be compared with the production process. For the educative process itself reveals to us that the other-person-to-be-educated is not nearly willing to submit himself to the plan, intentions and functional determinations of the educator who plans or constructs that process. He is rather closed, resistant and unpredictable. In true fact, we know little more than nothing about what part of our educational intentions materializes in the heads and hearts of the consumers. Yet this does not alter the fact that the most secret ideal of educational agents is to guarantee an undisturbed and undifferentiated flow from intention to fulfilment and from plan to implementation. In spite of the pledge of an active orientation towards the needs and the experiences of the learning subjects, didactics is, at its core, a search for the alchemistic formula for the betterment of man who cannot be allowed to be incorrigible - and certainly not in the face of a threatening annihilation of the human race. This otherwise secret intention receives its unvarnished expression by behavioural change technologists like B.F. Skinner, who explicitly uses the production concept when propagating the "production of automatic good behaviour" through manipulation of contextual contingencies (SKINNER, 1971).

This hidden intention is expressed with greater shame in the <u>concept of involvement</u>, which dominates the pedagogy-of-the-future. Involvement has become a kind of miraculous educational weapon. Involvement is no longer something which <u>happens</u>, but something which has to be created according to the rules of educational art in order to reach a political or any other objective. Pedagogical production has differentiated its task field. It is no longer restricted to the desired behaviour produced by the pedagogical operation, but education also has to create its own means of production namely involvement.

At this point, environmental educationists are

desperately veering off into a twilight zone. They have to rely on potent doses of those catastrophes which they want to counteract by means of their production of consciousness. They are condemned to "catastrophily", at least in the form of an adjuring imagination. Yet, as the example of Chernobyl shows, they have to rely on harder facts. And thereby, they irritatingly become the accomplices of the catastrophe-<u>makers</u>, to the detriment of their credibility.

However this is not sufficient. The ecological educationists fall short of the frame of mind which they want to install in their clients. Involvement would be the ultimate seriousness. Sloterdijk (SLOTERDIJK, 1986) speaks of the "culture of panic" which is not blind but sophisticated and realistic consternation. This culture does not fly but holds firm, it endures but refuses to take benefit from fear and finally to endow catastrophe with a sound meaning. Pedagogical calculations around catastrophe constitute one of the ways to avoid the ultimate earnest, to curb fear, to manage consternation to empower powerlessness. The pedagogy of catastrophe is a procedure by which one makes the unbearable bearable for oneself while imposing it upon the others. It comes down to a mere illusion of getting into action, and again, to the detriment of credibility.

There is one last fact which inevitably refrains ecopedagogy from realizing its intended practice. It has already been pointed out in Günther Anders' diagnosis made in the 1950s. According to him, the dilemma of modern man resides in his antiquatedness, "our inability to remain psychically up to date and well-informed about our production" (ANDERS, 1980, p. 15). "As temporal beings", we "are in disorder". We meander "as disturbed saurians amidst our apparatuses". Anders calls the "a-synchroneity of man with his world of products" the "Promethean gap". This is the gap between making and imagining, between doing and feeling, between knowledge and conscience - e.g. between the ability to destroy and the ability to mourn - and, above all, between the produced instrument and the human body.

> Because this gap really exists ; because we, as sensitive humans, still find ourselves in the rudimentary homeworkers' stage, whereby we can, if necessary, mourn a single person killed by

us, but have, as killers or producers of corpses reached the proud stage of industrial mass production; because the performances of our human hearts - our inhibitions, anxieties, precautions and sorrows are developing inversely to the extent of our deeds (i.e. are shrinking to the same degree that our deeds increase) - we are the most distorted, disproportionate and inhuman beings that ever have existed, provided the consequences of these gaps do not destroy us right away (ANDERS, 1980, p. 271 f.).

What can we, in the presence of such a disproportion teach or communicate to others ? Günter Anders actually states that the act of feeling enters also into the category of human ability. But even if some kind of crazy hope would lead to us to believe that we might be able to broaden our psychic capacities, this would never be amenable to a systematic educational activity. Not in the least because educationists take an equal part in antiquatedness as in the frenzy of survival described earlier. Therefore, Günther Anders does not refer us to the <u>curriculum</u> but to <u>exercise</u>.

Ecopedagogy - a failing practice? Yes! It must fail because of its internal contradictions:

1. it wants to produce ecological consciousness and ecological action while renouncing true ecological learning;
2. it wants to realize multiplicity through consensus in a programmed way;
3. it makes use of catastrophes, which it wants to help avoid;
4. it avoids the consternation which it wants to diffuse;
5. the broadening of psychic capacities can - if at all - only happen through experience and not by systematic transmission.

If "persuasion labour" and educational influencing are the opposite of ecological learning, then what could be the nature of a process whereby learning, thinking, meaning and competency of different kinds would be brought into balance? What might be the nature of a discussion which does not aim at unanimity and practical consensus? What does it mean if we would - to use the terms of Ivan Illich - stop in all earnest to try to exert influence? And what could we gain from such an attitude and from a non-educational discourse? This would mean to get up and stand with empty hands. With regard to this, Jean François Lyotard says what follows: "The elimination of the <u>educatable</u> third party equally belongs to the new perspective as well as the elimination of finality, truth and unity" (LYOTARD, 1977, p. 45).

I can not nor will decide here upon whether we should refrain from any operative intention in the actual world situation, and whether we ever would be able to do so. Nor can I decide upon the question whether the will to operate has become a kind of second nature, a basic social characteristic of industrial society. I rather want to ask what we can <u>gain</u> from non-educational, ecological learning.

If persuasion does not determine the <u>process</u> and consensus is not the <u>aim</u> of discussion or of a learning process, what then is the guiding idea? It would come down, then, to working out <u>differences</u> and to express and define one's own meaningful experience. This is no plaidoyer for arbitrariness and non-commitment, but, on the contrary, for good care and precision. This kind of discourse is not bound by <u>consensus</u> as a <u>product</u>, but by <u>respect</u> as a <u>condition of participation</u>. Respect is, to me, the first ecological virtue.

The commitment required by this kind of discourse can be circumscribed as "reflexive orientation" to oneself, the other and the object. I have to admit that I subsume a kind of hope here, which Hannah Arendt has worded in the form of a question : "Could not perhaps thinking as such... and without looking at the possible results and the specific content, be a part of the conditions which would prevent man from doing evil things or even predispose him not to engage in evil acts ?"(ARENDT, 1979, pp. 14-15).

Parting from the basic idea of differentiation and expression of personally felt meanings, one has to discard certain ways of speaking, thinking and acting which usually determine our educational actions : opposition, contention, outrivalling i.e. the art to beat another with one's own arguments, to criticize, to justify and also to make obstinate assertions. Instead, other acts gain weight : communication, story-telling, doubt, consideration, further questioning, admitting mistakes. I think the first type of acts impedes precise thinking and careful listening. Statements and counter-statements which are used to put through the "better argument", lose a part of their reasonableness due to the intention to win. The acts of sharing, doubting, considering and inquiring are however not competitive. In them, there is room and time for the specific, the strange and the controversial.

Furthermore, the perspective of a learning process without educational impulse does not allow one to provide oneself with a stock of arguments. We are really used to enter a discussion equipped with arguments. The stock - not to speak of a whole arsenal - of ready-made and repeatable statements is ill-adapted to the specific uniqueness of ecological learning, which is directed at experience and differentiation. It lacks actuality, is too unspecific and too unmistakable. The kind of truth which is strongly persuasive does not leave room for mistakes. An argument which is repeatable and situationally independent suffocates <u>curiosity</u> and makes <u>amazement</u> superfluous. Just like respect, however, curiosity and amazement are equally indispensable virtues for an ecological interaction with oneself, the others and the environment. On the other hand, these three virtues are less conducive to global insight than to the ability of <u>enduring strange situations and happenings</u>.

Supposing that these might be the contours of ecological learning, how then can we delineate an appropriate form of behaviour - or better an attitude corresponding to that kind of learning? If differentiation is brought to light, what is it good for? And whereto the advertising of personal meaning? For all this cannot lay the foundations of powerful action. In the face of differentiation, action power becomes feeble indeed. But I mean that uncertain action power is healthier for our present world than the tough version of action power. The bringing to light of differentiation is akin to the art of restraint. For centuries, we have witnessed the domination of the ability to effectively operate, to overcome and to control. It is possible that in our time, the art of letting things take their course and getting rid of the addiction to optimization has simply become a matter of survival.

Where differences are coming to the surface, there uncertainty is furthered. After centuries of the domination of knowing-for-sure, a kind of able non-knowledge seems to be of vital importance : the obstinate doubt, the tenacious search for the hiding places of the commonly accepted self-evidences, the awareness of the impossibility of deciding. Whenever the certainty of decision gets lost, caution will have to direct the course of action. The plaidoyer for differentiation is a plaidoyer for caution.

To advocate the expression of personal meaning, is to take the side of multiplicity. The right to equality has been perverted by the gigantic campaign of destroying culture, by the establishment of a uniform global culture which Pasolini, in his films, has called "consumism". This means that nature is recklessly thwarted, bereaved of its proper meaning, and devalued as a mere arsenal for the satisfaction of human needs. A centuries-old perversion of the right to equality, has to be brought back to balance by putting forward the right to inequality, i.e. by furthering multiplicity and open interaction.

Let us now turn to our second question : is the ecological movement an educational movement?

At the fifth international congress of Physicians for the Prevention of Atomic War in Mainz (BRD), I heard Peter Rühmkorf resume his own rather dark analysis of the political world-scene as follows : "It sounds damn fatalistic, I know ... But precisely here we reach the turning-point, where one asks us the most simple question : 'What can we do ?' - Our intrepid answer should be : 'Become more human!'"

"To become more human" is the educational program of the (new) social movements - although we may often be unaware of this.

Apparently, the related principle of non-violence, to which nearly all of the (new) social movements have subscribed, does not allow any other form of resistance than an educational or symbolic one. However, the program "To become more human", is confronted with the same dilemma as environmental pedagogy.

The response to a death-provoking technology must be an unconditional NO, independent of the question whether majorities vote in favour or against. For the possibility of a democratic, i.e. majority decision-making has been exhausted. (On the same basis, the death penalty was abrogated in the Federal Republic against the wishes of the majority of the population.)

The question is now whether the program "To become more human" does not convert the unconditional NO into a conditional one, namely a No which would be made dependent of a majority decision?

What could be the nature of a non-educational

and ecological practice? I here follow once more the ideas of G. Anders. Nuclear industry in both its forms - the military and the one called "peaceful" - is a killing-machine (Reactor plutonium is a potentially useful base for nuclear bomb plutonium) (LOVINS and LOVINS, 1981, p. 25 f). It has only one comparable predecessor in human history : the concentration camp (ILLICH, 1982).

Thus, Anders recalls the proposition, discussed but never realized among the allied forces, to bomb and bomb again the railroad tracks to the annihilation camps in Poland, in order to prevent the transport of new Jewish victims. Likewise, he says, we should effectively attack the official powers. He warns against the hope we might leave it at harmless and benevolent persuasion efforts or stick to symbolic educational actions. "No, our duties are more serious, then we have to hinder those short-sighted but amighty people who can decide about the existence or non-existence of humanity, we have to tie their hands... Those who deny this duty of prevention are equally guilty" (ANDERS, 1986). Anders thereby thinks of a sabotage of the supply roads or lines to the killing machines. His diagnosis states, that we, the people of central Europe, are the inmates of the present-day concentration camps, whose chimneys are not yet smoking, but which can be turned into a glowing hell from one day to another.
If Anders is right in his diagnosis - and I don't see why he should not be right - then the whole ecopedagogical emphasis really appears to be a gigantic self-deception, through which we as educators withdraw ourselves from the risks of a really effective resistance. But I confess : the radicality of such a demand makes me most helpless, not in the least because I lack the courage to engage in a non-symbolic variant of resistance.

Should not resistance contain a pre-image of good human life? Sloterdijk speaks of a twofold but incompatible citizenship (SLOTERDIJK, 1986a). The least we can do is to listen to the voice that does not only doubt our right of existence as educationists in the 1990s, but also refers to our part in humankind's guilt.

REFERENCES

Anders, G. (1985) <u>Die Antiquiertheit des Menschen</u>, München
Anders, G. (1983) "Sabotieren wir die Friedenssabo-

tierer!", Taz
Anders, G. (1986) "Zehn Thesen zu Tschernobyl", Taz
Arendt, H. (1979) Vom Leben des Geistes, München, Bd. 1
Baudrillard, J. (1982) Der symbolische Tausch und der Tod, München
Canetti, E. (1981) "Macht und Überleben" in E. Canetti (ed.), Das Gewissen der Worte, Frankfurt
Giesecke, H. et al. (1972) Politische Aktion und Politisches Lernen, München
Habermas, J. and Luhmann, N. (1978) Theorie der Gesellschaften oder Sozialtechnologie, Frankfurt
Heller, A. (1978) Das Alltagsleben, Frankfurt
Illich, I. (1982) "Das Recht auf würdiges Schweigen" in M. and R. Gronemeyer (eds.), Frieden vor Ort, Frankfurt
Lovins, A.B. and Lovins, L.H. (1981) Atomenergie und Kriegsgefahr, Reinbek
Lyotard, J.F. (1977) Patchwork der Minderheiten, Berlin
Skinner, B.F. (1971) Futurum Zwei, Reinbek
Sloterdijk, P. (1986a) Das Andere des Andern (unpubl. allocution in Neukirchen, Austria)
Sloterdijk, P. (1986b) Frankfurter Rundschau (Interview by F. Rötzer), Easter

Chapter Six
PEACEMAKING IN THE COMMUNITY, THE NATION, AND THE WORLD

Paul WEHR
Department of Sociology
University of Colorado
U.S.A.

1. <u>The Problem</u>
I wish to address what I see as a central problem of our time and suggest how education in its formal and informal dimensions can help to solve it. The problem is the absence of peace and security - within families, within communities, within nations, within the world community. Persons, groups, races, nations, and the global community have a right to live in relative peace and security, yet they rarely do so now.

A partial cause of this condition are those stresses Walter Leirman referred to in his opening address - which in the two decades since the establishment of the adult education training program at Leuven, have produced a world of increasing danger and insecurity at all levels. Internationally, the twin spectres of a nuclear inferno and a subsequent nuclear winter have haunted us with an ever increasing intensity. At the level of the group, conflict and tension have escalated, as around the world oppression is resisted and cultural identity is celebrated. A distant illustration is the struggle against apartheid in South Africa where behavioral violence mounts daily as structural violence is challenged. A significant, though more moderate conflict continues to evolve here in Belgium, where linguistic, religious, and ethnic divisions weaken the security of the nation. Despite the gains in intercommunity cooperation made since the separation of the Catholic University of Leuven into the Flemish one at Leuven and the Walloon one at Louvain-La-Neuve nearly two decades ago, Belgium continues to have serious unresolved internal divisions that weaken it.

At the personal level, climbing divorce rates,

sexual abuse, and increasing family violence in so many societies is bringing untold misery and loss to hundreds of millions of personal lives. In certain police precincts in the United States, for example, the largest percentage of murders involve people related to one another by birth or marriage.

As the world's human population increases in coming decades, competing for increasingly scarce space and resources, developing weapons of greater and greater lethality, it must for its own survival as a species grow in its ability to manage and resolve conflict at these different levels. This means not ignoring or suppressing conflict, but working with it toward outcomes creative for those involved. In short, masculus and femina must become peacemakers.

It follows then, that the knowledge and skills of making peace are vital resources for a nation's security. With its people knowing how to do it, a nation such as Belgium would be healthier and stronger internally, and better able to protect itself from internal and external threats to its security.

Assumptions
Certain assumptions underlie my thinking here. The first is that learning how to make peace has many dimensions. It is sometimes a formal learning activity going on within universities. At the same time, it can be an informal process of lifelong learning outside schools. On the one hand, it can be a practical exercise occurring in connection with a particular dispute. On the other, it can be a simulation in a classroom illustrating certain theoretical principles of conflict. Peacemaking can be an amateur activity in one's personal life within one's family, neighborhood, or workplace. Yet it can also be a professional activity with which one earns a livelihood ... witness the 3000+ participants in the Third National Conference on Peacemaking and Conflict Resolution meeting in Colorado this past June. Many of those participants were conflict resolution professionals - mediators, communication facilitators, arbitrators, counselors.

A second assumption is that peacemaking occurs at many levels. It is not just a condition between nation-states as we have traditionally conceived of it. One link between international, societal, and interpersonal peace is the individual. Through persons, the skill and inclination for peacemaking cuts across the various levels. The skill for making peace in the family, for example, is also likely to influence that person's attitudes towards international conflict and how his or her nation should resolve it.

Within persons' life experience, their peacemaking knowledge and skill emerge from and influence their major <u>social roles</u> (Figure 1). In those roles they interact with others whose peacemaking capability interacts with their own. Their respective peacelearning is mutually stimulating, producing a synergistic effect – a capacity, in the sum, greater than either could generate on their own.

Figure 6.1

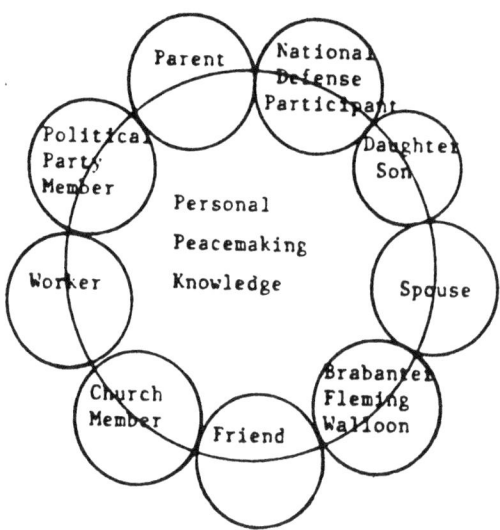

Peacemaking and social roles

Another way to view the interlevel/intercommunity link of peacemaking is <u>through institutions</u> – which are, of course, composed largely of persons. Institutions tend to operate at different levels of society simultaneously – the church, for example, or government. Such institutions, had they a conscious peacemaking mission, would influence policy in that

direction at many points in the socio-political structure.
    Yet another assumption underlying my thoughts is that <u>peacemaking is an unfolding process</u>. Just as learning how to behave violently or aggressively, or to make war, or to exacerbate conflict, is at least in part, learned behaviour, so too is the theory and practice of peacemaking and nonviolence. Like all learned behaviour, peacemaking depends heavily on <u>social invention</u> ... breaking away from traditional ways of doing things. It involves creating with synthesis and innovation, something quite novel in the way of human problem solving. One discovers new ways of making peace through historical encounter with the problem, a problem which is not solvable with existing ways of responding. One is <u>forced</u> to invent. I have recognized this process of social invention in a number of case studies I have done of nonviolent resistance movements. Such resistance in Gandhi's India (WEHR, 1979), Quisling's Norway (WEHR, 1984), Walesa's Poland (WEHR, 1985), and Reagan's America (WEHR, 1986a) reveals to us striking degrees of social invention in response to problems and condition which defied the usual violent responses. So while there may be a good deal of the systematic, the methodical, the repetitive in peacemaking, the genius of it may lie in the unpredictable, the inventive, the novel.
    <u>My final assumption is that</u> the university has an important role to play in the production and the transmission of peace knowledge. Most of peacemaking and peacelearning is, of course, taking place outside the university. But the higher academic institution has, at least in the ideal, special attributes (e.g. neutrality, impartiality, openness, spirit of inquiry and questioning) that make it invaluable for peacemaking.

2. Building a National Peacemaking Capacity

One moves logically from the conviction that peacemaking ability is necessary for national security, to the question of how that ability can be developed. Let me suggest how Belgium (and other nations by implication) might build such a capacity in their citizens, as a source of national security. There are three <u>types</u> of peacemaking to be developed.

Peacemaking in the Community

Negotiation and mediation

The capacity to mediate and negotiate disputes among family members, between different racial and linguistic groups, and in the workplace, would decrease the considerable social and economic costs of such conflict. The sheer psychic energy required to carry on such disputes, which too often result in gross injustice, resentment, and rancor is incalculable. A certain amount of that is inevitable in any modern society. It could, however, be substantially reduced by the training of persons in schools, churches, labor syndicates, industrial firms, and government bureaucracies in the practice of dispute resolution. Even concerning the national political system one must not be too quick to judge what is peace development and what is not. The negotiated creation of regional assemblies and governments for Wallonia, Flanders and Brabant may seem at present to have produced separation rather than integration, thereby weakening the nation. Yet such regional autonomies may ultimately strengthen Belgium by decreasing the sense of exploitation and inter-communal resentment felt by important segments of the population. Resolution of Belgium's political, ethnic and confessional divisions, in the long run, could be as much a success as Lebanon's has been a failure, if Belgians are diligent in learning how to make peace.

Nonviolent Action

A second dimension of peacemaking of national security importance is an increasing knowledge of nonviolent action (NVA), its uses, and its limitations within a society. I consider NVA to be a form of conflict management in that it is usually stimulated by a dispute or injustice, and is especially useful for those low-power groups in society (e.g. racial and ethnic minorities, working classes, unemployed, women, youth, peace activists) who may not have equal access to other ways of bringing about desired social change. Nonviolent action, whether it be a labor strike, a peace camp, a women's march, or a demonstration for jobs, increases the social solidarity within a nation in two ways. First, it reduces the violence and rancor that are often consequences of intense conflicts. Opposing sides learn how to get through those conflicts more or less peacefully. Second, in the longer term, it tends to increase social and economic justice within a socie-

Peacemaking in the Community

ty, and decrease coercion of some groups by others. This, too, strengthens a society by making it more equitable and tension-free.

Nuclear pacifism. We know an increasing amount about nonviolent protest and its influence on international and domestic conflict and violence. Citizens in Europe and North America, for example, protesting at the nuclear arms race, have clearly shown the peacemaking link between how they peacefully conflict with the policies of their national governments, and how governments (at least in the long run), learn to make peace with one another.

One can view this nonviolent activism of citizens as a <u>macromovement</u>. Collectively, nuclear pacifism grows through demonstrations, civil disobedience, and a great variety of modern communication methods.

> Such trends in the larger political system as modern communications development have permitted the essential process of networking. In Belgium, the nuclear pacifist network VAKA links national organizations with 200 local committees and tens of thousands of individuals. VAKA is both a coordinating body for the established peace organizations and an information network for political socialization of nuclear pacifists never before active. They thus gain experience in influencing policy and in defending their opinions in a public forum. (WEHR, 1986a, p.136)

One can also view nuclear pacifism as a collection of <u>micromovements</u>.

> ... expressions of rejection of injustice and irrationality. Nuclear pacifists, understanding the nuclear weapons state and the probable consequences of its continuation, are convinced that such a condition is unjust to them and their children, and (that the state is) irrational in its claim to defend (them).
> Perhaps our focus should be not on forcing nuclear pacifism into the established mold of collective action to better mobilize (the movement's) resources, but to explore new ways to help nuclear pacifists be more effective and more inventive (individually) where they are in the social system, in transforming the nuclear weapons state.

Peacemaking in the Community

(WEHR, 1986c p.142)

The real success of citizens' nonviolent activism will lie in their ability to integrate the macromovement activity (i.e. group and national protest) with micromovement action (isolated resistance by individuals). Group protest activities are important for movement impact, but no more so than the day-to-day steadfast resistance by individuals in their daily lives. My future research focus will be on this progressive integration of micro- and macro-action.

Poland. A most revealing illustration of the inventiveness and power of nonviolent action, both cooperative and individual, is the movement under way in Poland for the past two decades. This experiment in nonviolent social transformation has the most serious implications for international peace and security in Europe, the most insecure continent in the world. The Solidarity movement and its ultimate repression by the Polish state, were only events in a much larger nonviolent revolution which continues in Poland today. Solidarity signalled

> ... an eruption throughout the society of civic activity of immense diversity, ranging from the trade unions themselves to associations formed to halt pollution and to protect consumers (areas that had been monumentally neglected by the regime).
> ... In this burst of activity, the very ingredients of political life, having been pounded apart by forty years of totalitarian rule, now came together again in new and vital forms. The classic formula for revolution is first to seize state power and then to use that power to do the good things you believe in. In the Polish revolution, the order was reversed. It began to do the good things immediately, and only then turned its attention to the state.
> ... Its simple but radical guiding principle was to start doing the things you think should be done, and to start being what you think society should become. Do you believe in freedom of speech? Then speak freely. Do you love the truth? Then tell it. Do you believe in an open society? Then act in the open. Do you believe in a decent and humane society? Then behave decently and humanely.

Peacemaking in the Community

(SCHELL, 1986, p.60)

In a novel distinction between state (which has been left to those who control it) and society (transformed by the people), the Polish revolutionaries have invented social transformation processes with the most profound implications for security in Europe and elsewhere. One of the most important is that revolution can occur with little violence and slight risk of war. In the Polish case, both Solidarity and the Polish state restrained political violence during the 1980-81 period with remarkable effectiveness. I watched these restraints operate at close range with my own eyes (WEHR, 1985). They ranged from Solidarity's adherence to nonviolence, to the negotiations and mediation skills all sides developed during that time.

The Polish experiment suggests the untapped power that lies within societies to shape and defend themselves in ways that support rather than threaten human survival in the nuclear age. The Polish experience is valuable not only for the internal security of the Polish nation, but for what it may contribute to continental and global peacemaking.

We are led to wonder whether in the realm of international affairs and diplomacy there may not be a solution as unlikely in the eyes of the experts as Solidarity was - some ultima ratio beyond violence which the world is driven to employ, for reasons both pragmatic and idealistic, precisely because violence, the old ultima ratio, is now useless and bankrupt. If such a solution should be found, and if it should be employed to reunite a divided Europe, then it would be not only a counterpart of the Polish movement but a complement to it. Then Poland and the world escape from their plights along the same path.
(SCHELL, 1986, p.65)

Social Defense
A third dimension of national peacemaking is the training of a nation's people for social defense. Here national security is strengthened not so much internally as in response to possible external threat. A number of social scientists (e.g. ROBERTS, 1969 ; SHARP, 1985 ; GEERAERTS, 1977 ; MELLEN et al. 1985) have already done important work on the

theory of social defense. And a joint military-civilian working group has been studying Belgian social defense possibilities for some time now at the Université de Paix in Namur.

I suggested above, that a society which is more peaceful, equitable, and integrated internally, is better able to withstand attack from the outside. Social defense adds to that preparedness by providing a way for the entire population to become usefully involved in the nation's external defense. Citizens of Belgium say, would be involved in shaping a social defense policy, would be trained in it, and would carry it out if the need ever arose. Social defense would provide a more participatory defense policy in which citizens not in the armed forces would be active participants in their defense, not helpless victims of attack.

Nonviolent civilian resistance has been shown in a number of historical situations to be effective in protecting a nation's social and political institutions during military occupation (e.g. Nazi-controlled Norway), in resisting tyrannical regimes (e.g. the Philippines of Marcos), and in prohibiting coup d'états (e.g. Gaullist France). Such internal capability is an important part of a nation's defense strength.

Defense turned outward is necessary as well. Here, I would consider social defense as a part of a larger alternative defense strategy that would include rejection of nuclear weapons based on one's national territory, and a shift to what is now called non-offensive defense e.g. non-offensive weapons (GALTUNG, 1984) or an armed forces structure of small units defending limited geographical areas (ADC, 1983). Social defense by a population trained in nonviolent resistance would link with such alternative approaches to military defense in a policy that could well be more conducive to peacemaking and European security. It would involve the public more directly in national defense both as trained defenders, and as supporters of a national defense policy which is at the same time more native in its design and function, and less dangerous in that it does not rely on nuclear weapons.

3. Institutions for Peacemaking
In indentifying three types of national peacemaking knowledge and skill - negotiation and mediation, nonviolent action, and social defense - I promised

to suggest ways the development of such knowledge could be facilitated.

The most efficient way to strengthen the peacemaking capacity of people is to prepare them within the society's educational institutions. This could be done through new conflict management courses in both public and private denominational schools. It could be more widely done through adult education training programs developed by universities, labor syndicates, and municipal governments. For example, I am now developing a correspondence course in social conflict for the University of Colorado that will be available to adult students all over the U.S. It will include readings, simulations, audio-visual materials, and suggestions for internships and research projects.

In fact, as I said earlier, the university has the possibility to be a powerful peacemaking institution both in how it manages its own internal conflict, and in the peacelearning it offers its students. Let me illustrate using my own university, Colorado, and my community, Boulder. One reason the university, at least in my experience, holds great promise for peacemaking is the potential it has for cooperative effort with community institutions. An interesting experiment at the University of Colorado is the Conflict Resolution Working Group comprised of twenty faculty members from a number of disciplines including sociology, law, political science, geography, business, communication, and psychology. This is an experiment to learn if a multidisciplinary approach to conflict analysis and conflict resolution is possible. We studied our first dispute this past year, analyzing a local land use conflict. The disputants - government officials, landowners and lawyers and neutral third party observers, presented the conflict to us from their very different viewpoints. We then created four working groups of faculty, and each group formulated a multidisciplinary analysis and resolution strategy. We wrote a report (see WEHR and FITZSIMMONS, 1986), then discussed the paper and the value of the process with the participants. A striking revelation was that academicians and community people can interact productively in pursuit of conflict resolution. The hope is that this type of community-faculty and interdisciplinary interaction will grow into a permanent center for conflict resolution at the University for resolving local disputes more creatively.

Peacemaking in the Community

A second project linking community and university in peacemaking is the city of Boulder's Landlord-Tenant Mediation Project. With many students and transient people living in Boulder, it has more than its share of housing-related disputes involving housemates, tenants, landlords, neighbors, and police. The students and faculty of the Sociology Department's Concentration in Social Conflict are very much involved in the project both as trained volunteer mediators, and as researchers observing and analyzing mediator effectiveness. Social Conflict students are studying for degrees in Sociology, with a special emphasis on conflict analysis and conflict resolution. This leads them and their professors not only into housing mediation, but into other peacemaking activity in the community as well. They help organize peace action campaigns and projects such as the Nuclear Freeze, the Boulder-Jalapa (Nicaragua) Friendship Cities program, the Rocky Mountain Peace Center, the Sister Cities (Boulder-Duchambay, USSR) link, Medical Aid to El Salvador, the Community in Action (CIA) organized to protest at Central Intelligence Agency policy in Central America and its recruitment of students at the University, and other peace action designed to press governments to change violence-producing and war-threatening policies. Since professors and students are working together in both the classroom and community peace action, there is a healthy integration of theory, practice, and self-critique.

A formal knowledge base is essential for this integration of theory and practice. Academic courses must be rigorous, analytical, and objective in their identification of problem and solution. Our Conflict Resolution Monitoring Project has identified 850 university courses in conflict resolution being taught around the U.S. (WEHR, 1986c).

There must also be a database for researchers, teachers, students, and conflict resolution professionals to use. Thus we have begun building CONFLICTBANK, a computerized repository of all published materials on conflict analysis and resolution judged valuable for both theory and practice. Initially, CONFLICTBANK will contain only data in English but will ultimately expand to include other languages as well. Students will both use and add to the bank as they come through our courses and research projects. It will be a resource open to outside users by telephone and computer access.

Peacemaking in the Community

The University must also make peace within itself. From Sweden, it has borrowed the concept of "ombudsman", and has created a variation on that theme. The Ombudsman's Office at the University has become a multi-purpose problem-solving and conflict resolution center. Run by highly skilled professionals, it mediates, for example, disputes between professors and students. More rarely, it may mediate between a professor and the University, though such cases are normally handled by the faculty Committee on Privilege and Tenure.

For the most part, these different peacemaking efforts originated independent of one another and are only now beginning to find one another and cooperate. While my university is, I think, somewhat ahead of most large universities in its development and integration of peacemaking, it is by no means unique. Lest I mislead you, I should note that the University of Colorado and its environs are also deeply involved in military training, research and production. The nuclear weapons plant at Rocky Flats is only ten miles from my office. Reserve Officer Training Corps cadets march in uniform through the campus. And faculty at the Colorado Springs branch of the University recently voted overwhelmingly to urge a policy which permits secret research on their campus.

In my experience, the university is a most likely and congenial place for peacemaking to flourish. It is an institution relatively free from the social control of the marketplace and the government. It has a tradition of commitment to free and open inquiry, to experimentation with new ideas, and to support of basic human values and rights. It is also the training ground for a society's leaders. And not least important, every university is part of an urban community, so it is a natural meeting ground for community members, students, and faculty.

While the mixing of peace action, peace scholarship, and peace practice can be done well in universities, it must also occur in the other important social institutions where we live - schools, churches, government, the workplace. A nation must encourage formal and informal peacelearning in all of these places. It must support the growth of peacemaking professions and institutions at different levels.

A nation need not proceed without assistance in this. There exists a rapidly expanding peace science movement linking teachers, researchers, trainers, and practitioners in many societies. This movement ranges from the most formal, high-level peace institutes such as the United States Institute for Peace established by the U.S. Congress, to the independent trainers in nonviolence working in the schools, universities, churches, labor unions, parents' organizations, juvenile detention centers, and other social units of Belgium.

The tools of this peace science are conflict analysis, mediation, negotiation, social science research, diplomacy, communication facilitation, theory tested in practice and a praxis rooted in theory, and experimentation in developing nonviolent modes of resisting unwanted change and encouraging desired change. This enterprise is a science in the sense that it discovers principles or conflict behavior and devises a technology for limiting it to nonviolent, creative modes. The creators of this peace science are as diverse as their tools, ranging from university professors of highest standing in their respective disciplines, to children learning to mediate a classroom conflict.

Tying this growing enterprise together is a global network of literature, professional associations, personal travel from nation to nation, transnational research projects, international peace movements, and computer links. Increasingly this makes the peace knowledge base available not only to government and organizations, but to individuals as well.

My concluding point here is that there are many ways a nation can expand its citizens' peacemaking knowledge, from the highly formal and impersonal, to the very informal and personal. I would hope that as all nations look increasingly to their own resources and needs for their national security, that a peace-knowledgable citizenry will loom large in their thinking.

REFERENCES

Alternative Defence Commission (1983) <u>Defence Without the Bomb</u>, Taylor and Francis, London and New York

Boserup, A. and Mack, A. (1975) <u>War Without Weapons : Nonviolence in National Defense</u>, Schocken, New York

Galtung, J. (1984) <u>There are alternatives</u>, Spokesman, Nottingham, England

Geeraerts, G. (ed.) (1977) <u>Possibilities of Civilian</u>

Defense in Europe, Swets and Zeitlinger, Amsterdam

Roberts, A. (1969) *Civilian Resistance as a National Defence*, Penguin, Baltimore

Schell, J. (1986), 'A Better Today', *The New Yorker*,

Sharp, G. (1985) *Making Europe Unconquerable*, MA : Ballinger, Cambridge

Wehr, P. (1979) *Conflict Regulation*, CO : Westview, Boulder

Wehr, P. (1984) 'Nonviolent Resistance to Nazism : Norway, 1940-45', *Peace and Change*, Vol.X, n° 3/4

Wehr, P. (1985) 'Conflict and Restraint : Poland, 1980-1982' in Wallensteen et al. (eds), *Global Militarization*, CO : Westview, Boulder, 191-18

Wehr, P. (1986a) 'Nuclear Pacifism as Collective Action', *Journal of Peace Research*, Vol. 23, n° 2, 133-43

Wehr, P. and Fitzsimons, A. (1986) *Getting Theory and Practice Together : The Conflict Resolution Working Group*, Department of Sociology, University of Colorado, Boulder

Wehr, P. (1986c) 'Conflict Resolution Studies : What do we Know?', *Forum*

Chapter Seven
PEACE EDUCATION : LEARNING HOW TO TRANSFORM A LIFE-
WORLD THREATENED BY VIOLENCE

Walter LEIRMAN
Cath. University of Leuven
Belgium

What did the MUNDIAL MEXICO '86 have to do with peace and peace education ? At the first sight, not very much : international football is <u>game</u> plus <u>business</u>, and most of its protagonists declare that soccer has little or nothing to do with politics ...
Yet, Joao Havelange, the FIFA-president, stated at the opening ceremony in Mexico that he hoped "the Mundial would bring peoples and nations closer together, and promote peace in the world ...".
Thus - indirectly at least - the Mundial happening seems to be a peace promotion activity on a worldwide scene or even on a national level, as in Belgium, where the positive results united Flemings and Walloons in a temporary upsurge of common national pride. Yet, at the moment we were writing this paper, one of the quarter-finals to be played in Mexico City, was Argentina-Great Britain. And look, both the British and the Argentinian press, were talking of "the first confrontation between the two nations since the Falklands viz. the Malvinas war of 1982". Instead of a peace promotion activity, a soccer game might be viewed as the continuation of a war between two nations ... This reminds me of a statement made by Rinus Michels, the manager who prepared the Netherlands team for the 1974 World Cup : "Football is war, with other means but with the same objectives".

<u>Peace and peace education : complex and controversial realities</u>
Peace and peace education are complex and controversial realities. To begin with : the concept of peace is being linked in many minds to the <u>absence of war</u>, or, in a broader sense, to the <u>absence of</u>

large-scale violence. And according to the old Roman adage, the best way to prevent war is to prepare for it:"si vis pacem, para bellum". One of the most modern applications of that adage is the policy of nuclear deterrence between the Soviet Union/Warsaw Pact and the United States/Nato Pact. However, the upward spiral of nuclear armament is showing ever more the logical, moral and economic unacceptability of the deterrence concept. Johan Galtung, the Norwegian scholar who has been dealing thoroughly with the issues of war and peace, has been one of the first authors to distinguish between a so-called negative and a positive peace concept (GALTUNG, 1983). The first concept, sometimes indicated with terms like "minimal" or "threadbare peace" refers to the absence or the prevention of direct, large-scale violence. The second concept, also called "optimal" or "just" peace, refers to the prevention of structural violence, which takes the form of social discrimination, oppression and marginalization.

The negative or minimal peace concept is, in the end, based on the need of safety of social groups, nation-states and political blocks.

The positive or optimal peace concept is ultimately based on human rights and the striving for a just social and economic order. This concept is of a more recent nature, and one of the factors heavily contributing to its blossoming, has been the transition from colonialization to independence in the so-called Third World or, positively stated, the movement towards social, economic and cultural development of the Southern Hemisphere. Thus, a North-South dimension has been added to the East-West confrontation. In this spirit, the ancient Roman adage should be rewritten : "si non vis bellum, para pacem". If you want to avoid war, prepare for peace.

A further revelation has been the growing insight that peace is not only a matter of a structural (inter)national sphere, but reaches into the personal and functional life spheres of men as well. One sometimes talks of "small-scale peace", as the striving for a group and community life where conflicts are resolved in a non-violent way, which bears an analogy to "large-scale peace" where the actors are nations or large collectives. And to complicate matters further, one can also detect another dimension in the different ways of conceiving of peace : some people lay a heavy stress on stability, preservation or prevention, whereas others accentuate the need for either social reform or radical social change, i.e. the development of a new economic or political world system, etc. The first view is of a more static nature, the second one is rather dynamic. Given the difference between minimal and optimal peace, we shall further differentiate between a static-conservative and a static-preventive mode on the one hand, and a dynamic-adaptive and a dynamic-innovative mode on the other.

Our previous brief analysis has also made it clear that peace is a normative, value-laden concept related to different ideologies.

Thus, what has been called the "pax americana" is radically different from what has been called the "pax sovietica". The first one stresses values like personal liberty in a (neo)capitalist free market system, whereas the second one stresses social equality in a collective and guided or planned market system.

Let us now try to visualize all this in an encompassing scheme, which shows the conceptual complexity of the peace concept (Figure 1).

Figure 7.1

PEACE A CONCEPTUAL FRAMEWORK

		PERSONAL AND INTERPERSONAL LIFE-SPHERE	STRUCTURAL LIFE-SPHERE
MINIMAL OR NEGATIVE PEACE : THE ABSENCE OR PREVENTION OF VIOLENCE	STATIC CONSERVATIVE	personal safetey contracting	social-political safety contracting
	DYNAMIC ADAPTIVE	(re)conciliation	Pacification
OPTIMAL OR POSITIVE PEACE : CREATION OF A NON-VIOLENT CIVILIZATION BASED ON HUMAN RIGHTS	STATIC PREVENTIVE	personal rights declaration	social rights declaration
	DYNAMIC INNOVATIVE	non-violent interpersonal conflict resolution	non-violent social conflict resolution

We here unite the three aspects or dimensions discussed above : minimal vs. optimal, static vs. dynamic, and (inter)personal vs. structural. The latter dimension can still be differentiated further into group, community, nation, world region and global earth as Paul Wehr clearly indicates in his second assumption on peacemaking. In each cell, we name the basic type of action which is undertaken to realize that specific form of peace. The peace actions undertaken may - and often will - bear other names, of course. Thus, negotiations to reduce arms will either fall under the category of socio-political safety contracting or, when they constitute a dynamic-adaptive reaction to an ongoing conflict, they will take on the form of pacification. Furthermore, we want to stress the fact that (inter)personal peace bears only an analogy to structural peace : we are indeed dealing with conflict prevention or regulation, but more factors come into play when we move to the structural level : next to personal insights, attitudes and skills - which now play a less conspicuous role, we here are dealing with social structures, norms and rules, social instruments and means, etc. which will determine the (im)possibilities of preserving peace or overcoming structural violence to a high degree. Therefore, it is rather rare to see a realization of non-violent social conflict resolution.

Several types of peacemaking, like those mentioned by Wehr in his paper, can also be integrated within our conceptual framework. Thus negotiation and mediation belong to the conciliation or pacification category, whereas nonviolent action and social defense are expressions of a positive peace effort, and more precisely of non-violent conflict resolution at the structural level.

In view of all this, peace education both as a concept and as pedagogical effort, appears to be equally complex as the peace concept itself, and to some it is even utopian or entirely dismissible.

As with education in general, the views on peace education vary widely indeed and peace education is sometimes underestimated and sometimes overrated. From a negative or minimal peace point of view, peace education appears fairly irrelevant. Peace is seen here as a matter of politics, which - as von Clausewitz so poignantly states - comes down to a power game where values and ideals play barely any role. It is difficult to engage in a discussion or debate with such a point of view. One of our

colleagues once made the following comment : let it suffice to remind us of the contribution of education in national-socialist Germany from 1933 onwards ("Ein Volk - Ein Führer" ; superiority of the "Arian race") to the outbreak of the Second World War under Hitler's direction. There can barely be any doubt that Nazi-education corroborated war-mindedness in Germany. On the other hand, we should ask ourselves whether a radically different type of school and youth movement education in Germany would have prevented war - granted the possibility of its being accepted or tolerated by the political system.
Similarly, some adherents of the positive or optimal peace concept overestimate the possibility of peace education or of grassroots peace movements to influence defense policies and curb the (nuclear) arms race.

The peace movement as a New Social Movement
The advent of a positive or optimal peace concept is narrowly linked to the efforts of charismatic leaders and social groups who were confronted with heavy physical violence or structural oppression. Let us point here to Polish and French artists and intellectuals who founded the International Peace Council in 1947, to the non-violent liberation movement in India led by Mahatma Gandhi, to the Movement of American Negroes under the inspiring leadership of Martin Luther King, to Solidarity in Poland under Lech Walesa.

In Western Europe, the refueling of the nuclear arms race towards the end of the 1970s, has led to a fairly massive reaction against the deployment of new missiles in East and West, and by 1981 everyone was speaking of the "new peace movement as a large social movement". We also witnessed signs of such a movement in Eastern Europe, in North America and in Latin America.

In the same period, sociologists started a systematic analysis of what they called New Social Movements (NSM). They specifically referred to the Third World Movement, the ecological movement, the women's movement and the peace movement which, according to them showed marked differences to the "old" social movements like the workers movement of the second half of the 19th century.

Thus, a group of Dutch authors (VAN DER LOO, et al., 1984, p. 12 f.) point to three characteristics: the proclaimed values, the ways of social action and the type of actors promoting the movement. In terms of values, the NSM seem to orient themselves to the problems of the social "Überbau" or suprastructure, i.e. cultural issues and the quality and the nature of production rather than the "Unterbau" or infrastructure of production. Even though they often seem to act on single issues - like the implantation of a nuclear electricity plant - they profess a holistic view of man and society and stress ecological harmony, universal solidarity, and a sober, free and creative lifestyle. The well-known Frankfurt social scientist, Jürgen Habermas has made a similar analysis of the conflicts underlying the new NSM stating the following : "They do not concern themselves with the restoration of damages which the modern social state might repair, but with the defense and re-institution of a threatened lifestyle or with the realisation of new lifestyles" (HABERMAS, 1981, p. 161).

The new ways of action of the NSM show the following characteristics :

1. they are unconventional, like the "visits" by Greenpeace activists to ships which transport nuclear waste to the high seas;
2. they are single-issue-oriented, like the actions concerning "Harrisburg '79" or "Chernobyl '86";
3. they reveal a dissociative and sceptical attitude towards established social institutions;
3. they show very flexible and decentralized organisation patterns in the sphere of "direct democracy".

As to the actors, the analysts note that they tend to come out of the new, well-educated middle classes, are fairly young (25-35 years) and work in the "non-productive" sectors of society (education, health, social services). These actors can be further differentiated in three groups : the core leaders and promoters, the militants and the followers.

In fact, as A. De Geest has made clear in his study of NSM, we are witnessing here the advent of new ideological oppositions in society : productivistic economy versus ecological harmony, large scale vs. human scale, high-technological vs. alternative or humane technology (DE GEEST, 1984). Many analysts believe that these oppositions are superimposing themselves on the "old" opposition of socialism vs. liberalism.

In view of all this, we would like to point to the fact that present-day talk of "the peace movement in the world" is in fact a gross simplification. First of all, not all so-called peace organisations bear the characteristics of the New Social Movements. The "grassroots" movements, that have sprung up in several countries, especially in Western Europe, at the end of the 70s, clearly bear many of the characteristics of the NSM. Furthermore, there are differences as to the peace concept adhered to and as to ideology. However, a single issue like the installment of new Euromissiles in Western and, consecutively, in Eastern Europe, has provoked a wave of common action in the period 1980-84. Thus, in October '84, the city of Brussels witnessed its greatest demonstration ever - with 400,000 demonstrators representing practically all ideological sectors and organizations of Belgian society - including many adherents of "old" social movements.

Sociologists have been rather late in "detecting" the peace movement and the peace issue - but some of their analyses have brought us useful insights, and prevented an all too idealistic view.

From our educational point of view, we would like to ask a question, however, that is not often raised : do the new social movements have an educational meaning ? (DE AGUIRRE, 1986, p. 14). As far as the literature is concerned, we have found some answers to that question in the Federal Republic of Germany. This should not be surprising, because the FRG has become known for its "Bürgerinitiativen" (citizens' actions) since the 1970s, especially in the areas of environmental pollution, urbanization and nuclear energy. Thus, L. Von Werder talks about "everyday adult education" in an ecological perspective (VON WERDER, 1980), and M. Gronemeyer describes the "phenomenon of brave new learning" (dreistes Lernen) (GRONEMEYER, 1984). Those analyses make it clear that NSM have a double orientation : a <u>political</u> and a <u>cultural</u> one. Politically speaking, the NSM aim at the realization of concrete changes - such as the elimination of Cruise missiles from Belgian territory or the termination of nuclear energy for electricity production in Sweden or FR-Germany. Culturally speaking, the NSM are striving to realize changes in consciousness or in cultural or political behaviour - such as a peace mentality, non-violent behaviour or continued vigilance to violations of

human rights.
This brings us to the educational relevance of NSM. This relevance is (can be) both _internal_ and _external_. Internally, the NSM constitute a social and political _experimental learning field_, where participants can develop new insights, skills and social action patterns and may also learn to communicate and cooperate in a more effective way. Externally, NSM may provoke changes in their "target groups", i.e. politicians, social institutions or even the public at large - who can at least develop awareness and knowledge about the issues which are raised and the propositions that are put forward.

Education and the differentiated life-world
From what precedes, it should be clear that education may be _implicit_ or _explicit_. NSM - and other efforts at change - do not in fact have an explicit educative function. They are there to bring about change, and learning may be "a fruit plucked under way".

Explicit or systematic education - as in our third example of institutions offering new programs dealing with NSM-issues - aims however at bringing about learning results in a systematic way. And there we see a third educational relevance with the advent of the NSM : existing educational institutions are invited (or, maybe, forced) to offer new programs with new contents and new methods of teaching and learning. This sometimes happens in cooperation with NSM-members. Elsewhere, we have circumscribed education as "a process of systematical influence towards the realization of a valued individual and social life-project, i.e. a _goal perspective_ and an _action plan_ against a social background" (LEIRMAN _et al._, 1981, p. 21).

The central elements of the educative effort are therefore, the development of a human goal perspective and a concomitant action project. According to D. Wildemeersch , these are two basic elements of the human life-world, called, in his terms, _aspiration program_ and _action program_ (WILDEMEERSCH, 1985b, p. 217). Education should refer to and depart from the life-world of every human person. This consistency life-world constitutes a meaningful framework for the aspirations and the actions of every man and woman in the world. At the same time, this framework is imbedded in the larger social context, with socially accepted goals and <u>values</u> on the one hand, and socially accepted <u>means and instruments</u> on the other hand.

Aspirations and goals refer to the <u>reflection</u> side of our existence, whereas action programs and means belong to the <u>action</u> side of life. Reflection and action are both present at the "subjective" level of the individual person as well as at the "objective" level of the social context. This leads to the following scheme of the human life-world :

Figure 7.2

THE COMPONENTS OF THE HUMAN LIFE WORLD

	ACTION		REFLECTION
PERSON	action program		aspiration program
		contra-dictions	
CONTEXT	socially accepted means		social goals

The figure contains one element which has not yet been explained : in everyday life man seems to live "in harmony", i.e. there are no clear tensions between what he or she <u>thinks</u> with what he or she <u>does</u> within the "given" society. However, this kind of "inner peace" may be disrupted or even heavily attacked, either in a global manner or in a specific domain of life. A sudden economic crisis, an urbanization decision involving the necessity to leave one's house or a natural or man-made catastrophe may create a <u>growing contradiction</u> among the components of the life-world.

Let us note here that not only man's <u>consciousness</u> is involved here, but also his patterns of daily <u>action</u> as well as the <u>social context</u> in which he or she lives. This is the reason why we are talking here of <u>life-world</u> and not simply of consciousness.

If we look at consciousness alone, we know that people develop different <u>levels</u> of consciousness within their life-world. The well known Brazilian pedagogue Paolo Freire who developed both a theory of "conscientization" and a successful method of literacy education, describes three levels of consciousness : the "magical" or immersed level, the "naive" and the "critical-transitive" level (FREIRE, 1970). Using this and other frameworks - like the one of Berger and Luckmann (BERGER and LUCKMANN, 1974), the already cited D. Wildemeersch developed a three-level theory of the human life-world, and used this framework for a qualitative empirical research project, carried out under our supervision (WILDEMEERSCH, 1985b). Figure 3 contains a visual presentation of this theory.

Figure 7.3

LIFE-WORLD DEVELOPMENT : FROM SELF-EVIDENT TO CRITICAL

TYPE OF LIFEWORLD	MOTIVATION TO CHANGE	COMMUNICATION PATTERN	LEVEL OF OUTREACH	CONTRA-DICTIONS	REACTION PATTERN	EDUCATION GUIDANCE
SELF-EVIDENT	little motivation of resistance	daily small	inter-personal	latent	conforming	supporting or direct and substitutive
THREATENED	growing need motivation	dialogue	inter-personal and functional	manifest situational	reactive	from directive to cooperative
CRITICAL	growing competency motivation	discursive discussion	inter-personal functional	manifest structural	emancipative	supporting

Without being able to elucidate in depth each of the elements of the life-world model, we will try to give a brief but hopefully clear description :

   1. THE SELF-EVIDENT LIFE-WORLD : as the term indicates, people living in this type of life-world are conducting a ritualized existence where "everything is like it has al-

ways been". There is little motivation to change and one often shows resistance to new ideas and practices, the communication pattern is mainly composed of everyday talk using "cliché's", and the outlook or perspective of social interaction does not go far beyond the interpersonal life-circle of family and friends in the closed neighbourhood. Therefore, contradictions - which objectively exist - remain latent, and the way of reacting to the social context is conforming or adaptive. In such a situation, the educator will have reduced possibilities to influence people. He/she can either support the existing life-world or - from a "critical" point of view - apply a directive guidance style. The educator then determines the goals and methods of education, and often does things "in the name of" the educatee. He or she then acts as a "guardian" or a "substitute".
2. THE THREATENED LIFE-WORLD : external threatening events, like the examples cited above, may force people to gradually give up their self-evident patterns of thought and action. What we witness here is a growing need motivation - the feeling of a necessity of change - and a communication pattern which moves from the impersonal "they" and "it"-style to the personal "I" and "you"-style of exchanging experiences and felt meanings. Contradictions between the life-world components now become manifest, related to the concrete situation, and the pattern of reaction becomes rebellious or reactive. In this situation, the educator will have to switch from a directive leadership style to a more cooperative one, leaving room for dialogue and personal expression and initiative.
3. THE CRITICAL LIFE-WORLD : at this level - which has also been called "rationalized" - people develop new insights, new action patterns and come up with alternative solutions for the problems facing them. They develop "competency motivation" (GRONEMEYER, 1976), i.e. readiness for change on the basis of successful learning experiences, and they communicate with others in a discursive, argumentative way. At this level, contradic-

tions are becoming manifest at the structural level, and the reaction type of people are emancipative, i.e. they start developing alternatives to existing cumbersome dependencies. Here, the educator does not need to give much direction any more, but has mainly to support the educatee's efforts in an active partnership relation.

Our succinct explanation of the theoretical framework might suggest that a transition from the self-evident to the critical life-world should not be too difficult, or that "the higher educated people" all belong to the critical life-world. In their globality, both statements are clearly wrong. Wildemeersch's research (WILDEMEERSCH, 1985b), carried out in the form of repeated qualitative interviews, with 48 inhabitants of a region stricken by unemployment and environmental pollution in Belgium - half of whom were more or less actively involved in a community action effort of NSM-character - revealed that the majority of them were to be situated in the self-evident or between the self-evident and the threatened lifeworld. Only a few could be fully situated in the critical lifeworld.

How can we translate the life-world theory into a pedagogical theory ? If we understand education in the qualitative terms of our definition given above, it is clear that the educative process can take its full start only at the point of transition from the self-evident to the threatened life-world. In our process-theory of adult education, we have tried to capture the learner's process in terms of a spiralling growth process, moving from a CONSCIOUSNESS OF LEARNING NEEDS WITHIN A LIFE-SITUATION over A LEARNING ROUTE DECISION to SELF-DETERMINATION AND TRANSFER TO EVERYDAY LIFE. Within the self-evident life-world, education mainly consists of "learning how to function better in a given life-context". Bearing this in mind, we present an overall process-scheme of educative life-world development in terms of a "clover-leaf-of-four in motion", using thereby the components of Figure 7.2 (see page 106).

In the self-evident world, people need to <u>confirm</u> and corroborate their usual <u>action patterns</u> and their <u>everyday cliché-type thinking</u>. The same applies to the social context, which goes on celebrating its "normal" <u>rituals</u> and proclaiming its <u>stereotyped ideas</u> (e.g. "the good life in our democratic society").

Peace Education

To a considerable extent, several educational institutions (families, schools, socio-cultural organizations) make a continued effort to "optimize the personal and social functioning of people". In times and situations where contradictions between the life-world components are objectively small, this type of education seems adequate. Two remarks must be made here, however. First of all, education supporting the self-evident life-world will always

Figure 7.4

EDUCATIONAL LIFE-WORLD DEVELOPMENT FROM
A SELF-EVIDENT WORLD   TO   A   CRITICAL LEVEL
        I   II   III

	ACTION	REFLECTION	A	R	A	R
PERSON	self-confirmation	cliche-thinking	self-exploration	self-questioning	self-determination	critical self-analysis
	CD		CD		CD	
CONTEXT	ritual celebration	stereo-typing	contestation	goal-confrontation-	solidarisation	critical social analysis

fall short of its real potential. The main reason for this, as both Marxist and socio-critical theorists have regularly shown, is the fact that any given historical situation offers, at best, an incomplete realization of humankind's social and cultural potential.

Secondly, the stability of the lifeworld is regularly threatened by external, and sometimes by internal crises, which oblige people to at least question their habitual action and reflection patterns. Here, education can become a lever to positive change. This can happen both in an implicit way - as our analysis of the NSM has shown - and in an explicit way. People will be enticed to "walk untrodden paths", that is to <u>explore</u> new ways of action, to <u>ask questions</u> about their own insights, skills and attitudes, to <u>participate in social</u> action and pro<u>test</u>, and to engage in the <u>public debate over goals</u>

Peace Education

and means. Explicit or systematic education can offer learning opportunities in one or more of the aspects mentioned here, keeping in mind the changes in motivation, communication and reaction patterns signalled above. The threatened life-world is a life-world of transition, however - at least in terms of desirable development. The challenges to both people situated within it and to educators is to transcend its existential uncertainty and incompleteness. If such a transition does not succeed, a partial or total regression to the self-evident life-world will become inevitable.

A transition to the critical (or "rationalized") life-world implies acts of self-determination and critical evaluation of one's own personality and functioning. The criteria for that will be found in the new values and goals which will be developed on a societal (or community) basis in what Habermas (HABERMAS, 1981) has called "a dialogue free of power coercive". At the same time, there will be created new forms of solidarity and cooperation on the level of the social context.

Let us not be mistaken here : these things have to be learned, and both implicit and explicit education will have to make their contribution. The New Social Movements, and especially the environmental movement, have proved that such a process can be carried out with reasonable success.

The question may arise here whether life-world analysis and educative life-world development provide a global and unequivocal classification scheme for individuals and/or whole communities. The answer to this question is a differentiated one : within a given community or society at a given point in time, one will find present the three described levels or some halfway combinations. Furthermore, one person may find himself in different life-worlds, according to the sector or domain of human activity. Thus, it is not only imaginable but also true that, with regard to labour and work relations, one may be operating at the critical level, whereas in terms of war and peace, one may be situated between the self-evident and the threatened life-world. We have the clear impression that this is the case with some leaders and militants of labour unions in several European countries who operate according to the adage: "jobs and labour come first, peace is not high on our agenda. Let the peace movements deal with that."

Peace education as a form of critical pedagogy

Looking at the life-world scheme, many of us would tend to think that the actual, manifest threat to world peace through the arms race, and more specifically through the Euromissile-crisis, should have moved the vast majority of Europeans of East and West to the level of the threatened life-world. In this connection, Fiederle (FIEDERLE, 1982, p. 198) has remarked what follows : "Barely any theme is more suitable to the proposition : what may strike us all, is also of grave concern to every single person! ... However, an actual theme does not have to be of importance to everybody : subjective actuality first of all depends on one's own motivation, and not on public discussion." It is a fact that the nuclear arms race provokes feelings of deep anxiety. The West-German peace pedagogue F.J. Ensel (ENSEL, 1984) wrote a book on "peace engagement" and gave it a surprisingly adequate title : <u>Richtige Angst und falsche Furcht (Right anxiety and false fear)</u>. He describes a possible development from "suppressed anxiety over really experienced fear to political peace engagement". In this process-scheme, we can easily recognize the life-world theory described earlier.

The majority of people suppress the almost unbearable anxiety concerning the nuclear holocaust. According to Ensel, they should unlearn "false anxiety" and learn the "real fear". To explain the first form, he refers to S. Freud's theory of neurotic anxiety suppression, giving the following examples (ENSEL, 1984, p. 78 f) :

1. <u>negation</u> of the danger of an atomic war, of the degree of danger and of its real causes - all of which leads to evasive "flight"-behaviour;
2. <u>replacement</u> of a faraway and untouchable threat with close ersatz-objects, to which one can act aggressively;
3. <u>rationalisation</u> of feelings of powerlessness.

To overcome such feelings of anxiety and powerlessness, man needs to (learn to) engage in counter-experiences of true participation and self-determination. Therefore, one needs to create action fields, which have a starting point in everyday life, and where one can develop partial competencies - whereafter the scope of thinking and action can be broadened.

In such a way, one can learn to distinguish between false anxiety and true fear - the latter being related to both the objective threat of e.g. nuclear war and the personal consequences of action-for-peace.

Ensel also discusses the tasks of the educator(s) in such a process. He states that <u>educative group work</u> is the main method to be used. Work in such groups (self-help groups, action groups, etc.) can have the following meaning (ENSEL, 1984) :

1. it helps people to live with the anxiety of nuclear war;
2. it provides a basis for commonly acquired critical information;
3. it offers a support in the case of threatened isolation or counter-measures by the authorities;
4. it may provide small "action fields" which help to convert anxiety into productive action;
5. it may enlarge the social horizon and help people develop another type of social attitude.

Thinking both of the life-world theory presented and the conceptual framework of peace outlined above, we are convinced that Ensel made an important contribution covering aspects of the three life-world levels and also covering the range of minimal to optimal peace.

The stress on group work may be historically better founded than Ensel supposes. For, during the 40 to 50 years old tradition of group work, several models and methods have been developed which bear a direct relationship to peace, understood as cooperative conflict resolution. We especially point to G. Konopka's <u>social group work</u> model (KONOPKA, 1963) , to R. Cohn's <u>Theme Centered Interaction</u> (COHN, 1971) and to J. Fritz's <u>Interaction Pedagogy</u> (FRITZ, 1975).

However, a greater attention should be paid to the <u>structural</u> level of the peace concept, and to a <u>larger spectrum</u> of educative methods. By the latter, we mean that community methods of education - as used in community development - should also be taken into account, as well as an active engagement in non-violent conflict resolution at that level.

In accordance with our conceptual framework,

peace education covers at least four areas, both on an individual and a social-structural basis : safety education, reconciliation education, human rights education and conflict resolution education.

Especially the latter area is found missing in many peace education publications. We would like to add that both theory and practice of conflict resolution on a community level have become a major educational concern in the last 10 to 15 years. Witnesses of this development can be found in several projects and publications of community development (VAN DE VEER, 1981) on the one hand, and social dispute resolution (MOORE, 1984 ; WEHR, 1986) on the other. It is especially in this area, where the personal and the structural dimension of peacemaking meet, that we need to develop new theory in close cooperation with new practice. As educators, we need to remain conscious, however, of the difference between peace policy, peace action and peace education. Each domain has its own rationale. The rationale of peace policy is of a political-strategic nature, i.e. the mobilization of all possible means for the preservation or restoration of security (i.e. minimal peace) using thereby the instruments of social control and top-bottom power. Peace action has equally a politico-strategic rationale, but is oriented rather towards the creation of a new social order based on human rights and it generally uses instruments of nonviolent action and bottom-top power. Peace education has generally a communicative rationale based on the acquisition of critical insights, a cooperative attitude and personal and social skills, all necessary to decrease interpersonal and structural violence and to increase our capacity for constructive conflict resolution. Peace education is interactively linked to peace action and peace policy, but can never substitute them. It prepares for, anticipates and supports a peaceful life-world, but cannot by itself create it.

REFERENCES

Baert, H. (1983) 'Agogische draagkracht. Een aanzet tot operationele begripsbepaling', Tijdschrift voor Agologie, 12, 5-23

Beck, W., Smit, B. en Vogelezang, H. (1978) 'En toch beweegt het !', Marge, 2, nr. 12, 389-401

Berger, P. and Luckmann, Th. (1967) The social construction of reality, Allen Lane, London

Berkers, F. (1981) 'Geen reglementering, maar struc-

turering van leerprocessen. Methoden en technieken van politieke vorming', Vorming, 30, nr. 8, 434-45
Brookfield, S. (1981) 'Independent adult learning', Studies in Adult Education, 13, nr. 1,, 15-27
Cohn, R. (1971) 'Living-Learning encounters : the theme-centered interaction method' in L. Blank et al., Confrontation : encounters in self and interpersonal awareness, Macmillan, New York , pp. 245-72
de Aguirre, Ph. (1986) Leer- en vormingsprocessen in de vredesbeweging (mimeogr.), Leuven
De Geest, A. (1984) 'Nieuwe sociale bewegingen en de verzorgingsstaat' in J. Vrancken en E. Henderickx (eds.), Zorgen om de verzorgingsstaat, Acco, Leuven, 239-67
De Keyser, C.C. en Van Hoof, F. (1982) Vredesonderwijs. Theorie en praktijk, I.O.T., Brussels
Ensel, F.J. (1984) Richtige Angst und falsche Furcht. Psychologische Friedensvorbereitung und der Beitrag der Pädagogik, Fischer Taschenbuch Verlag, Frankfurt am Main
Fiederle, X. (1982) 'Von der Friedensbewegung zur Friedensdiskussion. Didaktische Überlegungen zur Thema Frieden in der Erwachsenenbildung', Erwachsenenbildung, nr. 3, 197-200
Freire, P. (1972) Pedagogy of the oppressed, Harmsworth, Penguin, New York, London
Fritz, J. (1975) Interaktionspädagogik, Juventa, München
Glaser, B.G. and Strauss, A.L. (1977) The discovery of grounded theory : strategies for qualitative research, Aldine Publishing Company, Chicago
Gronemeyer, M. (1976) Motivation und politisches Handeln, Grundkategorien politischer Psychologie, Hoffmand und Campe, Hamburg
Gronemeyer, M. (1984a) 'Das erstaunliche Phänomen des dreisten Lernen' in Gustav-Heinemann-Initiative (ed.), Bürgerrechte 1984, Stuttgart, 32-6
Gronemeyer, M. (1984b) 'Was kann die Erwachsenenbildung von der Ökologiebewegung lernen ?' in Beer, W. und De Haan, G. (eds), Ökopädagogik, Weinheim, 145-50
Habermas, J. (1981) 'Neue soziale Bewegungen' Ästhetik und Kommunikation, nr. 45/46, 161-5
Jacobs, D. en Roebroek, J. (1983) Nieuwe sociale bewegingen in Vlaanderen en Nederland, Leon Lesoil, Antwerpen

Konopka, G. (1963) Social Group work. A helping process, Englewood Cliffs, Prentice Hall

Lammertijn, F. (1981) 'Sociologie van sociale bewegingen', Leuven (cursus)

Leirman, W. en Vandemeulebroecke, L. (1981) Vormingswerk en Vormingswetenschap, Een agologisch handboek, Helicon, Leuven, Deel 1

Leirman, W. (1984) 'Vorming op weg naar solidaire zelfbepaling : een open procesmodel' in W. Leirman en L. Vandemeulebroecke (eds), Vormingswerk en vormingswetenschap, Een agologisch handboek, Helicon, Leuven, Deel 2, pp. 9-54

Leirman, W. (1985) 'Recente ontwikkelingen in de vormingswetenschap', Pedagogisch Tijdschrift, 10, nr. 6, 282-94

Lovett, T., Clarke, C. and Kilmurray, A. (1983) Adult education and community action : adult education and popular social movements, Croom Helm, London

Mezirow, J. (1977) 'Perspective Transformation', Studies in Adult Education, nr. 2, 153-63

Rozemond, S., Evers, F. et al. (1984) 'De Derde Wereld Beweging vanaf de jaren vijftig tot nu', Vorming, 33, nr. 8, 9-23

Siebert, H. (1983) 'Erwachsenenbildung zwischen individueller Lebensplanung, sozialen Bewegungen und Sozialpolitik. Ein Blick in die Vergangenheit', Hessische Blätter für Volksbildung, nr. 3, 199-206

Van Beugen, M. (1978) Relatiesleurelaars betreden het strijdperk. Een inleiding tot veranderkundig denken, Van Gorcum, Amsterdam

Van Buuren, H. (1978) 'Verschuiving naar yin in Nederland', Vorming, 27, nr. 1/2, 4-8

Van Den Abbeele, E. (1982) 'Zelfbeheer en kleinschaligheid. Voor een andere economie', De Nieuwe Maand, 25, nr. 6, 383-93

Van Der Loo H., Snel, E. en Van Steenbergen, B. (1984) Een wenkend perspectief? Nieuwe sociale bewegingen en culturele veranderingen, De Horstink, Amersfoort

Van Der Veen, R.G. (1982) Maatschappelijke aktivering van achterstandskategorieën, KU, Nijmegen, (Doct. Diss.)

Van Dobben-De Bruyn, J. en Frerichs, L. (1981) 'De methode Paulo Freire in maatschappelijk perspectief', Vorming I, 30, nr. 8, 423-33

Van Parreren, C.F. (1971) Psychologie van het leren, Verloop en resultaten van leerprocessen, Van Loghum Slaterus, Deventer, Deel 1

Van Steenbergen, B. (1983) 'Toekomst met vrijwillige eenvoud. Sterke aanwijzingen voor een stille revolutie', Vorming, 32, nr. 1, 7-29
Van Steenbergen, B. (1981) 'Hoe overleven wij de toekomst ? Alternatieve maatschappij-ontwerpen en hun consequenties voor educatie en arbeid', Vorming, 30, nr. 9/10, 477-87
Wehr, P. (1979) Conflict regulation, Westview Press, Boulder
Wilcinson, P. (1971) Social movement, London Cit. in W. Beck et al. (1978) 'En toch beweegt het!', Marge, 2, nr. 12, 389-401
Wildemeersch, D. (1985a) 'Ervaringsleren tussen vorming en aktie', Vorming Vlaanderen, 1, nr. 1, 55-75
Wildemeersch, D. (1985b) Ruimtelijke ordening in het perspektief van vorming en samenlevingsopbouw. Theoretische verkenning van aktuele tendenzen en exemplarische 'leefwereld'-rekonstruktie in de Rupelstreek, Katholieke Universiteit, Faculteit der Psychologie en Pedagogische Wetenschappen, Leuven (niet-gepubliceerde doctoraatsverhandeling)

Chapter Eight
MULTICULTURAL SOCIETIES IN NORTH-WESTERN EUROPE

Eugeen ROOSENS
Cath. University Leuven
Belgium

In nearly every country there are internal problems connected with interethnic relations or so-called communal disputes (GLAZER and MONYNICHAN, 1963 and 1975; CARDINAL, 1977; DE VOS, 1977; THERNSTROM, 1980; DOFNY and AKIWOWO, 1980; STACK, 1981; LEE and DE VOS, 1982). In many cases they are about ten sions between peoples, nations or ethnic groups that have been on the spot for a long time. During the last 20 years many disputes between indigenous groups and immigrants from alien regions have taken place in North-Western Europe. The famous phenomenon of immigrant workers is the well known label under which these problems appear in the media (MARTENS, 1973; ROOSENS, 1981; HAMMAR, 1985; MARTENS and MOULAERT, 1985).

In this context many worried observers, including a number of politicians, talk about the realization of a 'multicultural society'. Many leaders of non-indigenous minorities use this term. The word suggests that a new situation has arisen on account of the settling down in guest-countries of immigrant population minorities having cultural traditions which more or less differ from the local ones, and that it is advisable to acknowledge and to accept the cultures of these newcomers as well. People often say that this diversity contains wealth and holds promises, and that everybody has the right to maintain and to develop his own culture. Some want to make way for other religions; one propagates 'reciprocal' or 'bi-cultural education'; makes an attempt at realizing adjusted forms of community work and adult education, and one hopes to come to a gradual integration of alien groups, in such a way that this integration doesn't mean cultural assimilation (Roosens, 1982).

All this is still in an initial phase, and one gets the impression that a lot of problems can be solved whenever the authorities supply money and means in order to develop the higher mentioned provisions on a large scale, so that all immigrants and their children and grandchildren can enjoy these new institutions. At first sight the whole matter seems to be a technical problem : one has to bridge 'cultural-gaps'. However, upon scrutiny, the con concrete situation proves to be much more complicated.

As a matter of fact, the objective-apparent differences between the respective cultural traditions bring about considerable problems. In an initial stage of settling in a foreign neighbourhood, differences in language hamper the communication between the autochthonous and the aliens - if they do not make it entirely impossible. Clothes, social manners between men and women and between parents and children, eating habits and ritual obligations may undoubtedly provoke alienation and surprise and may raise hostility (ROOSENS, 1979b). The unilateral imposition of the local indigenous language upon children of foreign origin inevitably raises communication problems and the discrimination of children from among immigrant groups (ROOSENS, 1979c; GAILLY and LEMAN, 1982; HEYERICK, 1985). At this moment, those conditions have already been described in a number of studies and have been denounced in many manifestations. And in my opinion one is right in stating that the autochthonous majorities and the politicians who rule on their behalf, have neglected those aspects of reality in an almost incomprehensible way. One should take the cultural differences seriously, also on the level of the pure 'technical' problems they raise.

In my opinion the term 'multicultural society', as it is used in common life, covers other realities too. As a matter of fact a culture always is someone's culture. And in the case of the immigrant minorities, their respective cultures belong to people who, in the view of the indigenous population are coming from less-developed countries, or at least from underdeveloped regions of southern countries. Moreover, 'immigrant workers' are workmen, and therefore their life-style is not of high esteem, because of the way in which the life-styles and cultures are ranked in a hierarchical classification: there are higher and lower life-styles, and the ones of immigrant labourers are, according to the autochthonous judgement, classified at the 'bottom of the 'totem-pole', just like those of indigenous labourers (AERTS and MARTENS, 1978; ROOSENS 1979b, 1979c and 1982).

This hierarchy of people which also co-determines the hierarchy of life-styles, is determined by a system of relations that is much more embracing and broader than the national reality of the respective guest-countries: in the international context countries occupy an hierarchical rank that generally is in proportion to their political economic power. By this fact alone, they are assigned a low rank, by a kind of international consensus. Moreover, everyone is aware of the fact that these immigrants, who accept jobs that are discarded by most of the 'nationals', are not likely to belong to the better situated socio-economic strata in their homelands. And this is a second factor that assigns a lower rank to the immigrants in virtue of the universal classification system of the guest-countries. Nobody can escape this hierarchical division in terms of respective status, not even the autochthonous inhabitants. And immediately one accepts it as normal and natural fact that the 'foreigners' of the immigrant workers type, including their children, are ranked in the lowest social category, i.e. in a class located lower than the one of the lowest-ranking autochthonous people (REX and TOMLINSON, 1979).

Added to all this, there is the fact that a number of immigrants are strikingly different in phenotype : one can distinguish them by their physical structure, and more exactly by the dark colour of their skin. By this the life-style likely to be appropriate to them is completely and definitely classified as lower. Almost all over the world, the so-called racial factor has appeared to be an element with a strong hierarchy-promoting effect (BANTON, 1983).

In North-Western Europe, as in many other places all over the world, phenotype, socio-economic position and life-style or culture start to refer to each other or start to symbolize one another on the common hierarchical scale of values.

Those who speak of the realization of a multicultural society ignore this hierarchy. He or she who propagate multiculturality as a 'must', either are naive, diplomatic or may be very brave, because this person is diametrtrically in opposition to very strong and extensive 'social' dynamics : for social promotion is not given away as a mere present. The generally established ethics of the majority states, as far as others are concerned - are that social promotion has to be merited. Thus, the acknowledgement of the so-called culture of immigrant employees as a culture that is fundamentally equal in value to the autochthonous one, ipso facto means that you grant a social promotion to the 'foreign workers' themselves, as a social category, and in many cases as a 'racial' category too. For broad strata of the local population, this is all the less acceptable, because in their view, also within the autochthonous communities themselves, social promotion is accompanied by a clear <u>change</u> - and often a well perceptible change in the lifestyle and in the sub-culture of the one who gets the promotion (ROOSENS, 1979a). In terms of the local social system, it would be perfectly logical that a successful foreign worker, supposing that he merits promotion, switches over to a 'higher' form of culture, and thus more and more assimilates himself to the autochthonous. That is why even the highest placed political leaders look for 'the solution' to many problems in the direction of naturalization, a 'solution' that is also suggested in 'the language of the common people' of some extreme-right political groups. A good immigrant is an invisible immigrant.

Yet this local system of values and system perceptions is confirmed by other factors.

To all indiginous people it is clear that the immigrants too are out to obtain prestige-goods : many buy glamorous cars, are bent on domestic appliances, on modern personal comfort and on gadgets, and thus are not averse to a lot of local cultureproducts. In doing so, they bear out the opinion of the local population which states that the true direction immigrants should take is one of a total modernization, and thus of a total absorption into the local, more advanced system (LEMAN 1982; CAMMAERT, 1985).

Looking from the outside, the children of immigrants, much more than the members of the first generation themselves, spontaneously go in for 'modern' life if they are given a choice. The youngsters are averse to the droll habits of their parents, they wish not to go to the Koran-school, they are bent on 'freedom', on a new recreational world, and appreciate fashionable clothes and the eating habits of their contemporaries from the majority groups. This seems to be an additional reason to admit that the endeavour to a multicultural society is a fallacy of a few singular individuals, rather of a 'left' signature (LEMAN, 1982, CAMMAERT, 1985; AUBERT, 1985).

An observer who watches the phenomenon of migration as unbiased and as closely as possible, will have to admit that not all statements of the vox populi are unfounded. It is clear that immigrants come to the North in order to better their financial position and gain the prestige that goes along with it. It is indisputable that many migrants who go back on holiday to their region try to make an impression with their cars and a series of prestige-goods that belong to a dream-world in the homeland. It is also correct that the so-called second generation perceives many aspects of the 'home-world' of their parents as behind the times and does not want to return to that world anymore. This turning in a certain direction in the field of material culture and technical achievements, comfort and security, manifests itself on numerous places all over the world.

Now when migrant-organizations and their indigenous sympathizers talk about the preservation of the 'own culture', they cannot possibly mean that one should transfer the Berberian-Rif mountains or the Souss-valley to Brussels. Or that one would like to start living here like in a village near the Black Sea (ROOSENS, 1985a). Moreover, the real problems experienced by children or migrants in adapting themselves to French-speaking or to Dutch-speaking schools seem to be not insurmountable. From a technical point of view one is able to change from one culture to another within a few generations. Indeed, the basic problem one meets, if one wants to introduce a multicultural society, is not situated here. When a group of immigrants or descendants of immigrants avowedly claims the right to a culture of their own, this claim often is accompanied by an attitude of opposition to the majority groups. The loyalty to the own culture is almost never just a technical-expressive matter, a self-evident continuation of what one did in the past (BARTH, 1969; LEVINE, 1973; PATTERSON, 1978; ROOSENS, 1986). Often the claim for a cultural identity includes a disapprobation of some values the majority holds, such as the equality of men and women; the autonomy that is granted to young people, especially young women, in the choice of a wedding-partner; the freedom of thought and opinion; the relative sexual freedom ... a lot of young people enjoy, etc. This disapprobation of values which, in North-Western Europe, are seen by many as a sign of rational behaviour and moral liberation and emancipation, is perceived by a lot of autochthonous people as a symptom of backwardness and 'medieval' mentality. Especially when immigrants appear radically to reject as 'immoral' and sinful procedures which the majority view as acceptable or even priorities, there is a chance not a few members of the majority refuses to tolerate foreign organizations on their own soil, by which, in their opinion, hopelessly outdated, 'primitive' conditions could be institutionalized. And that even happens with means that largely come from the majority ... When one is confronted with Islam fundamentalism, the reaction is even more severe. One does not accept that foreigners come to condemn or to proselytize the autochthonous people on their own territory (BASTENIER and DESATTO, 1985).

Something that makes the whole matter of the multicultural design even more incredible, is the fact that in a number of cases, the right to have a culture of their own, is claimed by young grown-ups, children of immigrants, who have partly moved away from their parents' culture and who have lost to a large degree continuous contact with the culture of the land of origin. These are frequently militant young people, young people who have gone through a phase of almost total identification with their contemporaries from the majority groups, and who have not infrequently consciously rejected the styles of living of their parents - but who have become disillusioned by the fact that neither the indigenous youth nor the local employers want to accept them as equal. They have converted this expulsion into a return to their own <u>ethnic</u> self-definition, whereby features of their own culture often are handled and manipulated in a rather arbitrary and fragmentary way, in order to separate and distinguish themselves for the autochthons (LEMAN, 1982).

With this preceding phenomenon in mind, one comes to the conclusion that the claim for the preservation and the extension of the own culture almost never is a neutral or technical matter. At the same time it also is, and perhaps not to an inferior degree, a claim to be acknowledged as fundamentally equal. It comes down to a claim for a certain autonomy, and thus for political power too, even if it were just via the suffrage at the municipal level.

Multicultural Societies in N.W. Europe

This public recognition as an entity that has the right and gets the means to be 'different' on a territory which autochthonous people perceive as theirs, seems hard to realize. The rhetoric of high demands that is carried on by some ethnic youth organizations, is not of a kind to make the claims put forward clearer and more acceptable to the dominant public opinion. All in all, the autochthonous people perceive it as if support and recognition are being asked for the maintenance and the promotion of values and institutions which seem to be outdated, or which do not belong to the guest-country.

The integration of ethnical groups that prefer to remain on their own comes about more strenuously in Europe than in the United States of America (FARELY, 1982) or Canada, because of the fact that most European guest-countries don't perceive themselves as immigration-countries. They think and feel about themselves as consisting of the 'authentic', rightful claimant sections of the population who have settled down on the territory for centuries. These 'real' inhabitants can tolerate foreigners on their territory, but these foreigners never really belong there, unless perhaps after long years, if they totally 'adapt' themselves, and in that way become invisible and cease to be strangers. And in contrast to a lot of immigrants in the United States, most immigrants in Europe are not eager to become naturalized citizens of the guest-country. Migrants coming from E.E.C. countries look upon it as superfluous, since they are 'Europeans'; and most immigrants from Northern Africa and Turkey perceive naturalization as a definite abandonment of their intentions to return, or perceive naturalization as desertion and disloyalty to their own family and people.

The situation outlined here, which has existed already for years, has become even more complicated since the full outbreak of the economic crisis, due to a general feeling of shortage on the labour market and in the sector of the social services. Without serious research being done this subject on an international level, one gets the impression, based on all sorts of indications that in a lot of sections of the population and in very different socio-economic circles, the conviction has grown that 'foreigners' have become an unbearable nuisance, because of the fact that they take, in an unacceptable way, advantage of our social services. Moreover they would make up a permanent threat to our security.

The behaviour of some figures and political groupings, especially in election times, gives a strong impulse to these feelings (PLENEL and ROLLAT, 1984; Cahiers de Sociologie.., 1981; LORIEN et al., 1985; TRÄNHARDT, 1985). Besides no one can deny the fact that there are problems. Migrant youth is indeed affected most by unemployment (MARAGE and LEBON, 1982).

In addition to all this, one has to take into account the considerable diversity that exists among the so called foreign workers. Italians for instance do not all want to be identified with Moroccans or Turks, and to Turks from the cities the Turks from the country-side seem backward. Moreover, one can observe big differences between individuals : some members of the first generation for instance are very capable of change and modernization and thus will want a secondary school training for their daughters, while others think secondary education is not for women. Some people of the second generation think that one should spread the immigrants preferably on a geographical basis, so that gossip and excessive social control do not prevent them from developing themselves according to the rules of the 'modern times' and not infrequently these young people prefer to mix with the autochthonous youngsters, rather than to limit themselves to their own ethnic circle. But one also meets with young people who act very demandingly and who think their autochthonous contemporaries are of little interest.

Still a set of other elements usually escapes the less-informed public's attention, because they are not perceptible or visible at once, in view of their predominantly psychological nature (DE VOS, 1975; EPSTEIN, 1978).

The fact that many immigrants of the first generation do not sympathize with the idea of evolving in the circles of the surrounding majority, is not only connected with language problems and social barriers, but also with the intention many foster deep inside - but that may never materialize or only much later - to finally return to their region of origin. The majority of the first generation has invested economically as well as socially and psychologically in their homeland. Migrants measure their success or failure against the situation in the homeland, using the norms of the homeland. The migrant population of people who come from the same region constitutes a kind of platform in the guest-country. In other words, the first generation remains strongly oriented to the homeland. This fact certainly does not urge them to penetrate - socially and culturally into the autochthonous circles.

With the children and young adults of the minority groups, who have grown up in the guest-countries, the feelings and the investments are structured differently, if you look at them from a social point of view : the references to the region of origin of the parents are minimal in most cases; but culturally one finds, also among the second generation, authentic and often unconscious links to the system of their parents, and psycho-ethnically many of them keep identifying themselves with their 'origin' and in doing so remain loyal to their parents, family and people. This ethnico-psychological belonging can manifest itself in political activity, though this is not necessarily so. Many migrants of the second generation disappear in the streets and the public life within the majority, but remain who they ethnically are by descent in the intimate circle and at home (LEMAN, 1984).

Within the first as well as within the second generation these psychological feelings of bondage to the previous generation and the mythical past of their origin constitute a dynamics one should keep in mind when you want to understand the implantation of minority groups in the guest-countries of North-Western Europe (DE VOS and ROMANUCCI-ROSS, 1975).

If one keeps all the foregoing considerations in view, one will understand that the realization of a multicultural society is a very complicated task. Nothing, or almost nothing, can be done in the perspective of a harmonious society unless <u>both sides</u> are willing to acknowledge one another as 'different' but nevertheless humanely acceptable. This implies the abandonment of racist attitudes, the acknowledgement - at least on the pragmatic level - of the factual multiplicity of cultures, which inevitably supposes a certain cultural and ethical realism; this also includes that one accepts the competition on the labour market of people who technically and juridically remain 'foreigners' and who wish to remain so. The immigrants, on their side, will have to realize that it is impossible to realize exactly what they hope for themselves.

The means to realize a multicultural society, which in fact is a multi-ethnical, a multiracial and equal society too, are hard to find.

Still it seems to be worthwhile and realistic to

strive for the realization of a society model which makes a harmonic co-habitation of various ethnico-cultural categories and groups possible. The return by force of E.E.C. foreigners to their homelands is an absurdity, and the wholesale expulsion of non-E.E.C. immigrants and their children is a political and ethnical improbability. A forced remigration, even if it only concerns non-E.E.C. residents, would be in flat contradiction with the positions proclaimed by the European authorities.

We are not entitled to outline the concrete policy concerning the introduction and the implementation of a multicultural society. There is always a big gap between reality and ideal. In my opinion nobody is able to draft scientifically founded policy rules in the matters of collective decision-making. But we can call attention to some facts and make a number of suggestions.

1. In many texts, documents and studies that do relate to our problems, and especially in the political discourse, various aspects of reality are continually mixed up. The migrant culture of the first generation is often assimilated with the culture of the homeland, whereas sometimes there are substantial differences. In the cultures of all migrants shifts have occurred; some immigrants are far 'more progressive' on many points than their relatives who stayed behind, while others have missed many of the recent changes in their region of origin, and thus turn out to be more conservative than their previous fellow men. And when the children of migrants talk about their 'cultural identity', they talk of something else than their parents. The policy-makers should acquire differentiated views on these realities, otherwise it might be possible that one goes astray with the best of intentions, or that one is guided by the tendencies among migrants that are the most vocal.
2. If one wants to realize a harmonic society, it is of course a necessity to let information about all groups involved flow through the whole system. The responsible authorities will have to initiate and stimulate carefully executed studies, and will have to inform the whole population of school-children and the teaching staff who are in charge of their training in the framework of a justified and

planned construction of knowledge. All kinds of officials, people within the mass media and political leaders too should get the chance of training themselves this way.
3. As experiences elsewhere in the world prove, providing information is not sufficient in order to develop a harmonious society; information is a necessary but not a sufficient condition. Also, in a country like Belgium, the intercommunity conflicts show that a good knowledge of the culture of the others does not necessarily entail good relations (HUYSE, 1981). In so far as we have insight in today's world scene, it seems to be the exception that ethnic groups, as groups, start to appreciate one another. But one meets many individuals who admire this or that trait in the culture of another people. The relations between ethnic groups are almost never solely connected with matters of cultures or life-styles, they are always connected with power-relations on the political and economical level as well. The relative status of ethnic groups or categories and of individuals from these different camps, always plays an important part. Thus one notices that children from the minorities are not inhibited or favoured by the relative size of difference between their parents' culture and the one obtained at school in the first place, but by the way the family of origin experiences the way it is incorporated in the guest-society. Children from 'paria' or 'outcast'-groups have less success at school than their counterparts from groups with a nearly identical origin, but whose parents were able to settle down in a less discriminatory or oppressing context (OGBU, 1978; VAN DEN BERG et al., 1983; FOYER-STUURGROEP, 1985; LEMAN, 1985; OGBU and MATUTE-BIANCHI, 1986).
4. If one touches matters of an intercultural nature, one immediatly touches matters of relative-status relations as well. No one can assert that an absolute conformity between the inhabitants of a country is necessary in order to maintain peace in a society. But it is undoubtedly a problem to policy-making when some social categories or groups, within the framework of the presentday world, land in an obviously inferior situation and when society promotes a rather avowed ethnic stratification.

One who wants to prevent or to limit such a process, will of course have to act on many levels at the same time, but certainly should not lose sight of school education and continuing education of the migrant-children. For the school constitutes one of the few places where policy is able to assert itself, in order to break through stereotypes and to impart to children and young people from all ethnic categories or groups, a minimum of mutual appreciation and tolerance. Training, moreover plays an important part in the determination of the chances one gets in later socio-economic life.

5. Centres for adult education can play an analogous part with regard to their public.
6. There are lots of parallels to be drawn between the situation in which most less well-off immigrants from non-E.E.C. countries find themselves and the system many colonized regions have known until the late fifties (REX, 1973). Just think of the 'carte d'évolué' the Belgian colonial authorities promised to the Africans who were able to prove that they were capable of approximating to the life style of the whites. One finds, just as in the colonial period, an evolutionistic perspective of culture : the culture of the guest-country is judged as being superior on all points. Also the invisible, but socially very real border between autochthonous people and the less possessing immigrants reminds us of the colonial situation, where the lowest ranked white-man - at least in his own opinion - was still worth more than the highest 'risen' black.

Of course one finds differences too. In the meantime, a different power-relation between nations and a different public international system of ethics have developed. At present, minorities being oppressed can appeal to the world's conscience and to international authorities that did not exist in former times.

But all in all, many members of the majority groups see themselves as being superior to their opponents from the minorities. The inequality between people seems to be a 'steady directive' which one does not abandon unless one has no choice, or unless one views it as a means to be better than the others.

REFERENCES

Aerts, M. and Martens, A. (1978) Gastarbeider, lotgenoot en landgenoot ?, Kritak, Leuven
Aubert, R. (ed.)(1985) L'immigration italienne en Belgique. Istituto Italiano di Cultura - Université Catholique de Louvain, Brussel - Louvain-la-Neuve
Banton, M. (1983) Racial and ethnic competition, Cambridge University Press, Cambridge
Barth, Fr. (ed.) (1969) Ethnic groups and boundaries : the social organization of culture difference, Little-Brown, Boston
Bastenier, A. and Dassetto, F. (1985) "Organisations musulmanes de Belgique et insertion sociale des populations sociales des populations immigrées" in Revue européenne des migrations internationales, Vol. 1, 1, 9-21
Cahier de sociologie et d'économie régionale (1981) Critique régionale 10-11, Recherches sur l'immigration, Editions de l'Université de Bruxelles, Brussels
Cammaert, M.-Fr. (1985) Migranten en thuisblijvers. De leefwereld van Marokkaanse Berbervrouwen, Universitaire Pers - Van Gorcum, Leuven - Assen - Maastricht
Cardinal, H. (1977) The rebirth of Canada's Indians, Hurting, Edmonton
De Vos, G. (1975) 'Ethnic pluralism : Conflict and accommodation' in G. De Vos and L. Romanucci-Ross (eds), Ethnic identity : Cultural continuities and change, Mayfield, Palo Alto, 5-41
De Vos, G. (1977) 'The passing of passing : Ethnic pluralism and the new American society' in G.J. Direnzo (ed.), We the people : Social change, Greenwood Press, London, 220-54
De Vos, G. and Romanucci-Ross, L. (eds) (1975) Ethnic Identity : Cultural continuities and change, Mayfield, Palo Alto
Dofny, J. and Akiwowo, A. (eds) (1980) National and ethnic movements, Sage, Beverly Hills
Epstein, A. (1978) Ethos and identity : Three studies in ethnicity, Tavistock, London
Farley, J. (1982) Majority-minority relations, Prentice Hall, Englewood Cliffs
Foyer-Stuurgroep, Bicultureel (1985) Vier jaar Foyer-bicultureel te Brussel. Een tweede evaluatierapport, Foyer, Brussel
Gailly, A. and Leman, J. (eds) (1982) Onderwijs, taal- en leermoeilijkheden in de migratie,

Acco, Leuven
Glazer, N. and Moynihan, D. (eds) (1963) Beyond the melting pot, MIT-Harvard University Press, Cambridge, Mass.
Glazer, N. and Moynihan, D. (eds) (1975) Ethnicity : Theory and experience, Harvard University Press, Cambridge, Mass.
Hammar, T. (ed.) (1985) European immigration policy, University Press, Cambridge
Heyerick, L. (1985) 'Problemen van migrantenkinderen en hun leerkrachten in het Vlaams basisonderwijs' in A. Martens and F. Moulaert (eds), Buitenlandse minderheden in Vlaanderen-België, De Nederlandsche Boekhandel, Antwerpen, 103-13
Huyse, L. 'Political conflict in bicultural Belgium' in A. Lijphardt (ed.), Conflict and coexistence in Belgium : The dynamics of a culturally divided society, University of California, Berkeley, 107-26
Lee, Ch. and De Vos, G. (1981) Koreans in Japan : Ethnic conflict and accommodation, University of California Press, Berkeley
Leman, J. (1982) Van Caltanissetta naar Brussel en Genk. Een antropologische studie in de streek van herkomst en in het gastland bij Siciliaanse migranten, Acco, Leuven
Leman, J. (1984) Integratie, anders bekeken, Cultuur en Migratie, Brussel
Leman, J. (1985) 'The Foyer project : A Brussels model of bicultural education in a trilingual situation', Studi emigrazione, XXII, 78, 253-66
Le Vine, R. and Campbell, D. (1972) Ethnocentrism : Theories of conflict, ethnic attitudes, and group behaviour, Wiley and Sons, New York
Lorien, J., Criton, K. and Dumont, S. (1985) Le système Le Pen, Epo, Antwerpen
Marange, J. and Lebon, A. (1982) L'insertion des jeunes d'origine étrangère dans la société française. Rapport du Ministre du Travail, Président du Haut-Comité de la population et de la famille, La Documentation française, Paris
Martens, A. (1973) 25 jaar wegwerparbeiders. Het Belgisch immigratiebeleid na 1945, Sociologische onderzoeksinstituut, Leuven
Martens, A. and Moulaert, F. (eds) (1985) Buitenlandse minderheden in Vlaanderen-België, De Nederlandsche Boekhandel, Antwerpen
Ogbu, J. (1978) Minority education and caste : The American system in cross-cultural perspective Academic Press, London

Ogbu, J. and Matute-Bianchi, M. E. (1986) 'Understanding sociocultural factors : Knowledge, identity and school adjustment' in Social and cultural factors in schooling language minority students, Evaluation, dissemination and Assessment Center, Los Angeles, 73-142

Patterson, O. (1978) Ethnic chauvinism : The reactionary impulse, Stein and Day, New York

Pienel, E. and Rollat, A. (1984) 'L'effet Le Pen'. La découverte, Le Monde

Raad der Europese steden en gemeenten (1985) Dokumentatie van de internationale conferentie 'Multi-cultural society at local level', Noordwijkerhout

Rex, J. (1973) Race, colonialism and the city, Routledge and Kegan Paul, London

Rex, J. and Tomlinson, S. (1979) Colonial immigrants in a British city : A class analysis, Routledge and Kegan Paul, London

Roosens, E. (1979a) Cultuurverschillen en etnische identiteit. Aspecten van het ontwikkelingsvraagstuk, A.B.O.S., Brussel

Roosens, E. (1979b) 'Désavantages et discrimination : la question des immigrés en Belgique', EEGrapport, Studi Emigrazione, 16, 54, 229-303

Roosens, E. et. al. (1979c) Omtrent de achterstelling van immigranten in België, Acco, Leuven

Roosens, E. De cultuur van immigrantenkinderen (thema-rapport), Conferentie 'Kinderen van Migrerende Werknemers', Raad der Europese Gemeenten, Rotterdam

Roosens, E. (1981) 'The multicultural nature of contemporary Belgian society : The immigrant community' in A. Lijphardt (ed.), Conflict and coexistence in Belgium, University of California, Berkeley, 61-92

Roosens, E. (1982) 'Etnische groep en identiteit. Symbolen of concepten?' in A. Van Amersfoort and H. Entziger (eds), Immigrant en Samenleving, Van Loghum Slaterus, Deventer 99-122

Roosens, E. (1985a) 'De sociaal-culturele structuur' in A. Martens and F. Moulaert (eds), Buitenlandse minderheden in Vlaanderen-België, De Nederlandsche Boekhandel, Antwerpen, 31-44

Roosens, E. (1985b) Towards a multi-cultural society? Raad der Europese Steden en Gemeenten, Noordwijkerhout

Roosens, E. (1986) Micronationalisme. Een antropologie van het etnische réveil, Acco, Leuven

Stack, J. Jr. (ed.) (1981) Ethnic identities in a

transnational world, Greenwood Press, London
Thernstrom, S. (1980) Harvard encyclopedia of American ethnic groups, The Belknap Press of Harvard University Press, Cambridge, Mass.
Tranhardt, D. (1985) ''Buitenlanders' als voorwerp van Duitse ideologische belangen en ideologieen' in A. Martens and F. Moulaert (eds) (1985) Buitenlandse minderheden in Vlaanderen-België, De Nederlandsche Boekhandel, Antwerpen, 289-305
Van Den Berg-Eldering, L., De Rijcke, F. and Zuck, L. (eds) (1983) Multicultural education : A challenge for teachers, Foris Publications, Dordrecht-Cinnamison

Chapter Nine
MULTICULTURAL EDUCATION AS A TASK OF ADULT EDUCATION : OBSERVATIONS FROM CANADA AND THE FEDERAL REPUBLIC OF GERMANY

Joachim H. KNOLL
Ruhr University Bochum
Federal Republic of Germany

A number of reasons - of a personal as well as of a societal nature - have enticed me to deal with the present subject on this as well as on other occasions. I myself have been raised in a culturally mixed region in the border-zone between Germany and Poland. Today, I am actively interested in the situation of the Danish minority in the province of Schleswig-Holstein and its development of cultural autonomy and identity. And I have also observed elsewhere in the Federal Republic the activities of ethnic minorities who have over a longer period of time realized their integration such as the Polish groups in the Ruhr area.

As objective-societal impulses, I can point to the great waves of migration after the Second World War and the problems of migrant workers in all western industrialized nations.

On the basis of both my personal biography and social sensibility, I have always tried to be open to models and concepts of multicultural education. This applies especially to my experiences in Israel, in Canada and in East Asia, i.e. countries with ethnically mixed populations who in part tend towards assimilation and in part to integration.

I agree with E. Roosens when he complains about the lack of linguistic precision in multicultural matters and when he states that more is at stake here than a mere battle of words and concepts : in discussions of educational policies as well as in seemingly scientific debates one often uses 'synonyms' which do not cover the same meanings. He gives the following example :

> The same terminological vagueness and linguistic confusion is encountered in the writings

about 'guest workers', the 'second generation', 'bi-cultural education' and so on. At a recent EEC colloquium (May, 1982), I noted that a Belgian governmental minister spoke about a 'multi-ethnic society', a 'multi-cultural community', and 'multi-cultural education', without having any difficulty at all with the use of these terms : the eminent speaker obviously considered them synonymous. Other speakers who were professionally involved in 'bi-cultural' or 'multi-cultural' education did the same (ROOSENS, n.d., p. 2).

This complaint is repeated on several other occasions (ROOSENS, 1985 and n.d.). For the sake of differentiation and justice, we have to add however, that several attempts at clear definitions have been made, e.g. at the congress of the European Society for Comparative Education in Würzburg (FRG) in 1983. These definitions and propositions have proved to be helpful - even for the practice of adult education itself (MITTER et al., 1985). In this connection, I want to point especially to the precisions formulated by O. Anweiler and F. Kuebart in a comparative analysis of multicultural education in Canada and the Soviet Union (ANWEILER and KUEBART, 1985, p. 219).

On the basis of the Canadian experience, I adhere to a concept which relates multicultural education to the retention of language and cultural traditions by ethnic minorities, giving them the right to their own cultural identity without barring the road to integration through isolation and group egoism i.e. through ethnocentrism (ANWEILER and KUEBART, 1985). We therefore want to repeat once more that multicuralism can barely be developed in countries pursuing the politics of assimilation : there, language and culture can only be maintained in relatively closed, ethnocentric groups; they are lively only in remote corners and suffer an increasing wear and tear in society at large (1).

Looking at our theme from the perspective of "adult education and the challenges of the 1990s", I express the hope that the realism of our present time has led to a sensibility which does no longer trust the political media messages right away. I hereby leave the question whether the opposition of educational optimism and reformism on the one hand and social anxiety and uncertainty on the other hand is rightfully made. Talking of political messages, I want to give again an example from the Federal Republic of Germany : in spite of high immigration rates, the statement is still made that the FRG is not an immigration country and that the problem of integration is therefore a marginal one. To me, such a statement is clearly contradicted by the actual situation, yet it is publicly applauded - as a recent article in the renowned <u>Frankfurter Allgemeine</u> (18.1.1985, p. 12) has shown.

To begin with : <u>the awareness</u> that multiculturalism is becoming an important task in the Federal Republic has become apparent in both the educational sciences and the practice of adult education. This awareness does not correspond, however, to an equivalent degree of scientific expertise. To state it in simple terms : in the Federal Republic, the actual level of research and knowledge concerning multiculturalism is by and large deficient. This situation clearly differs from that of countries with original ethnical minorities, such as Canada or Belgium (ROOSENS, 1985, p. 1), where the national state derives its legitimacy from the constellation of both ethnic integration and ethnic identity.

Furthermore we can state that comparative education has taken up the topic of multicultural education in its research repertory. This also applies to the FRG, with this distinction however, that the focus of attention is directed to other countries and not to the problems within the country itself (2). As to Canada, its educational research has reached a high standard in the domain of multiculturalism. This is especially true of the provinces of British Columbia, Alberta and Ontario, whereby the University of British Columbia (Vancouver) and the Ontario Institute for Studies in Education (Toronto) have developed a clear profile (MALLEA et al., 1979, Start here, 1984-5). But it still remains true that the optimistic phraseology on multicultural education tends to create an image of harmony which is not to be found in social reality. Thus, intregration partly fails because of the treatment of 'visible minorities'. Two researchers, Vincent D'Oyly and Kogila Moodley, who belong to the 'visible minorities' themselves, have criticized this treatment, especially since signs of a 'positive stigmatization' have become apparent in recent years. Apparently there is no lack of experiments and propositions to help the 'visible minorities', e.g. through a special quota-representation in the sector of the public services (KNOLL, 1987).

Multicultural Education

On the whole, one can state that comparative education has taken up the subject of multiculturalism with prudence and perception, whereas adult education has been clearly lagging behind.

There are, of course, monographs about subjects like 'The Turks in the Federal Republic', 'Continuing education of migrant workers', 'Socio-cultural problems of the second generation of migrant workers', etc. Yet, these publications rather aim at drawing clear borderlines and do not contribute much to integration. The science of adult education has barely discovered this problem area - and the first efforts were made from the perspective of diagnosis of deficits and target group orientation.

Thirdly, I want to state that, contrary to the science, the practice of adult education is taking new initiatives towards multicultural education. Here again, those countries which have focused on immigration as legitimate ground for nation-building, have taken the lead. This applies e.g. to Israel, which tries to realize the integration of North African Jews through the Tehila-project - Tehila meaning 'Glory' in Hebrew (TSIVION, 1983). In its turn, that project has a radiating effect upon the much less publicized efforts with Druses and Arabs in the country, which were analyzed by Eitan Israel of the Hebrew University. Similarly, we can point to the exemplary MOSAIC-project in Canada, aiming at the professional integration of ethnic minorities in the Canadian labour market (KNOLL, 1987).

In what follows, I want to look at tasks and desirabilities in the area of multicultural adult education. I thereby want to keep a critical eye on the good example of Canada as well as on the reticence in the educational policy of the German Federal Republic.

First of all, let us remark that multiculturalism does not seem to present any problem in border regions inhabited by linguistically mixed populations (KNOLL, 1986). Bilingualism does not create any demarcation, let alone isolation - bilingualism is accepted as a current and more or less normal principle. It is desirable for multilingualism and even total bilingualism to become a primary concern of adult education, as has been stated on several occasions.

Thus, the Danish minority in the province of Schleswig-Holstein controls an educational service system covering almost all needs; there is a vast network of schools and voluntary organizations, and a residential folk high school (Heimvolkshochschule) in Jarplund provides the ideal service which corresponds to the renowned Danish concept of the communitarian 'folkelig højskole'. The formal political and separationist controversies have been overcome, the Danish minority of Schleswig is represented in the parliament of Kiel whereas the German minority in Denmark is connected to the Danish 'rigstag' through a parliamentary institution (KNOLL, 1986).

Far more difficult, however, is the integration of immigrant workers, because, as we have already indicated, the official policy tends rather towards a segregational position and depreciates the immigrant workers as a transitory phenomenon determined by economic necessities. If we discard that kind of a position, then adult education has first of all to provide intregrational support. This kind of support is especially offered to the Turkish immigrants whom one can classify as a 'visible minority' in the Federal Republic. On account of their outward appearance, their religiously based system of family hierarchy and their cultural customs, the Turks are perceived as 'outlandish', and they offer an eloquent example of the 'interaction between discrimination and integration' (SILBERMANN, 1986, p. 9 f) (3).

What kind of measures could spur on adult education to contribute more to the integration of immigrant workers ? The ultimate goal cannot be, of course, assimilation, nor should it be, in the light of the program of multiculturalism.

To start with, the linguistic barriers have to be overcome - and the folk high schools are indeed offering numerous courses, with titles like 'German as a foreign language' or 'German as a second language'. A parallel to this is found in Canada, where numerous courses of 'English as a second language' (ESL) are offered. Yet, the acquisition of linguistic communication abilities cannot be the only objective here. Courses of this kind should at the same time provide 'country-knowledge' and further the comprehension of the new social environment. Furthermore, educational and recreational institutions in the area of youth work and adult education have to see to it that the linguistic and the cultural identity of immigrant workers is maintained and that they are not thrown into a no-man's-land :

not yet German - no longer Turkish. The measures of integration and reintegration exemplify this dilemma (UNESCO, 1985) (4).

On the other hand, the German population has to be prepared for an acceptance of immigrants which is not arrived at through tolerance alone but through knowledge. Up to now, there have been a few attempts at bridging the gap between Turks and Germans, but they are of a secondary importance and differentiated according to social class.

I have to refer here to the Canadian approach, which has now reached a phase of intensive discussions under the title Equality now (DAUDLIN, 1984). This publication defends the right to cultural autonomy and identity in a culturally mixed society and pleads for the retention of language as well as for a proper system of linguistic and cultural education. This means that where the population voices the desire and where it is quantitatively feasible, educational institutions for ethnic minorities have to be provided. All this is based on the principle of bilingualism, which has to a large extent been realized indeed. I notice similar tendencies in the Hispanic population of southern California where, contrary to the American assimilation policy, the cultural rights of the Spanish-speaking population are invoked. 'Equality now' aims especially at the integration of 'visible minorities' and more specifically the black population of Canada and the Asiatic groups. The attempts - which we were able to observe ourselves - to bring more members of these 'visible minorities' into positions of public office have been met with skepticism from the side of representatives of these groups and have been criticized as acts of 'positive discrimination' (KNOLL, 1967).

If I rightly judge the Canadian situation, then we can discern two tendencies on the part of ethnic minorities : on the one hand, the attempt to assimilate oneself as quickly as possible into the Canadian society - and thus, the Germans are said to speak nothing but English right from the gangway of the airport of arrival - and on the other hand the expression of the need for cultural and linguistic identity in relation to the country of origin - which is fulfilled mostly by churches and leisure-time organizations. And thus it happens that activities of that kind, which divulge cultural traditions and spread forms of leisure among the new environment, open up the borderlines around ethnical minorities and have a cross-cultural effect. Concretely : festivities organized by Italians or Germans are not simply attended by Italians or Germans, but by interested people from the different ethnic minorities living in a given area. I could observe such a cross-cultural effect especially in the MOSAIC-project and at the university campus in Vancouver.

However, these almost ideal examples of multiculturalism should not make us blind to forms of racism and discrimination which exist in Canada, as well as in the Federal Republic. In West Germany, one should expect a greater prudence and liberality in the contact with 'migrant workers' - given the burden of our war-history. In Canada, the racism is directed against Pakistanis and people from India - whereby Nazi language is used. Some people will be quick to remark that every immigration wave has been met at first with rejection, which then was reversed into acceptance during the second and third generation. This is certainly true of those who fit into the WASP-image (White, Anglo-Saxon, Protestant). And in a different way, the same can be said of the Federal Republic : those 'guest workers' who came from southern West-European countries - and are mostly Catholic - do encounter less difficulties with integration and acceptance than those who come from other countries.

With regard to Canada, I would like to draw the following general and somewhat simplified conclusion : there is an awareness as well as an action program of multiculturalism which manifests itself in the educational system, and there is a clear federal support for 'Canada multiculturalism', not in the least through a ministry which is active both on a provincial and on a national level. Canadian adult education is taking numerous initiatives to promote integration and acceptance - as is witnessed e.g. by the Welcome Houses in Toronto. On the other hand, there is a certain discrimination towards the 'visible minorities' which they themselves experience and disavow.

Let us now turn our attention again to the situation in the Federal Republic. We have already indicated that the ethnic minorities in border regions of the FRG do not present any serious problem. In Schleswig, bilingualism is as self-evident among the Danish minority as is their cultural orientation towards neigbouring Denmark. This is equally true of the school system, of adult education and of the churches. Both the national and the provincial government reached binding agreements with the Danish government regarding the status of these minorities right after the Second World War.

Yet, we are dealing here with a more or less autochthonous ethnic minority, whose history and language is closely linked to Germany and Denmark. There is no parallel here to the situation of those minorities who were attracted to the Federal Republic on economic grounds. And it should be repeated in all clarity that the Federal Republic cannot deny being an immigration country, whose task it is therefore to promote multiculturalism. This does not only mean that educational measures have to be taken, but likewise that the right to full citizenship has to be guaranteed after a certain time (5).

We have also noted that there exist clear differences of status and mentality among the immigrated ethnic minorities, and that the Turks constitute a problematic group, comparable to the North Africans in France, Belgium and the Netherlands. Furthermore, we already know that educational practice reveals a good number of provisions, whereas science, and especially the science of adult education, has been really hesitant to tackle this problem. The curricula for future adult educators do not contain the topic of multiculturalism at all. At best, there is some room for 'problems of foreigners'. As we know, the science of adult education in the FRG boasts a high standard of professionalism and expertise, whereby curricula for the training of adult educators are derived from the general framework for M.A. programs in education, established by common agreement in 1970 (VATH, 1984).

In the meantime, several modifications of those curricula have been made, but the issue of multiculturalism has not yet been incorporated. Likewise, a list of research areas in adult education does not make any reference to multiculturalism - although 'international adult education' and 'comparative adult education' are mentioned. The same applies to the available handbooks and glossaries - and that at a time when comparative education had already taken up the subject (WIRTH, 1978 and DAHM, 1980).

The training programs for future school teachers show a different picture however. Thus, the University of Hamburg was the first to install a postgraduate program for teachers of grammar schools and lower secondary schools who teach many children of migrant workers in their classes. Other institutions have followed this example.

Talking now of desirable developments and possible strategies, we wish to point out first of all that we see the best chances for an institutional multicultural adult education mainly in the area of 'informal education'. In more fashionable terms, one could also speak of 'alternative' education in contrast to 'institutionalized' adult education. The advantage of such a strategy resides in the fact that it offers a free forum for communication and discussion and refers the acquisition of cognitive skills and knowlege to the background. Looking at some alternative adult education institutions that I know of, I detect some structural changes in the fields which have not yet been recognized by traditional institutions. The folk high schools are mainly used as centers for the acquisition of knowledge, whereas alternative institutes function as opportunities for communication and for personal, almost familiar get-togethers. In the youth centers - mainly an instrument of extra-curricular youth education - such forms of informal education are already put into practice, e.g. in the youth centers (Häuser der offenen Tür) in Hamburg. Next to this, a new type of leisure center has been created, which has thus far received little or no attention in the discussions about adult education and youth work : we are talking here of audio- and video-play centers with all kinds of electronic and other types of gadgets (KNOLL, 1984, 1986). Today, youngsters as well as adults of both German and foreign origin, meet in such play centers - which on the one hand constitute a variant of the 'leisure industry', while on the other hand they are used as centers of informal adult education.

On the occasion of a visit to the alternative 'meeting point' Kum & Luk in Cologne by our students and staff, a female visitor to that center made the following division of the field of adult education : "When I am looking for knowledge, I go to the folk high school. When I am looking for social contact, then I come to this communication center." In short, if one wants to acquaint oneself with citizens of other ethnic minorities, one will find that such alternative and communicative provisions are best suited for the purpose. However, this does not free institutionalized adult education of its task to mutually inform immigrants and natives of their respective cultures.

This applies especially to a special kind of

illiberality in religious matters, furthered by an unspecific distance from religion as such. At first sight, this seems to be a paradox - but it is not. Many people in the Federal Republic keep a distance from faith and religious practice, or use religion as a lever to political demands. In the confrontation with people of other religions, however, they express a secular kind of orthodoxy which one would not expect in such a form. Thus, religious distance and sturdy self-righteousness seem to determine one another, and this causes considerable suffering to those who do not belong to the 'official' religions of our country, such as the Turks (GERBAULET, 1986).

Let us stay for a moment within the institutional context before moving to the content area. Just as there are Koran-schools - and without discussing their contrapuntual function - it should equally be possible for the ethnic groups in the Federal Republic to develop a concomitant school and adult education system. The Portuguese minority disposes, for instance, of specific educational provisions carried out by the 'Caritas' organization. Yet, those measures should not exclusively be directed at acquiring linguistic competencies but offer one possibility, among others, to explore a new world.

Just as there is a Judaic folk high school in Berlin and a broad research program on Judaism in Heidelberg and Duisburg, as there is a Danish folk high school in Jarplund, it should also be imaginable that Turkish or other minorities create educational provisions for the promotion of personal and cultural identity of their youth and adult population, which are derived from their cultural heritage. Why should a Turkish folk high school in Berlin or Hamburg be impossible ?

One day, multiculturalism will receive its institutional realization in adult education. We should also include here the media as informal agents of adult education. In the meantime, the press selects its news items mostly according to the principles of notoriety and deviance of foreign youngsters and adults, whereas television offers a program in foreign language entitled 'News from the home country', which is well-intended but marginal and often uninteresting.

In this respect, Canada deserves a special mention again. In Toronto, there are media stations addressing ethnic minorities the whole day long.

From such an example one could conclude that the extension of 'foreign' programs would imply a special program for each minority group. Moreover, cablevision could make it possible to realize encounters in well-determined areas.

With regard to the contents of multicultural adult education, we have already mentioned a few aspects of cognitive transmission and communicative encounters. But first of all, information of a mutual nature should be intensified. To take the example of the Turks : they should get to know more about the Germans and Germans more about the Turks, and this regarding many topics. We mention here demographic development, the economic situation including unemployment, the educational system and its possibilities for further integration and professional mobility, the family structures and hierarchies, the religious attachments and conditions, the cultural traditions, music and leisure. When we look at the programs of institutionalized adult education, whether state-sponsored or private, we find little of this multicultural catalog : neither the Turks nor the Germans are well 'served' in this respect.

Of course, the objection is made that educational barriers and resistance thresholds exist which cannot be quickly overcome. This may be true of the first generation, but certainly not of the second generation, whose members are fairly well acquainted with the system of (continuing) education, even in its intricacies. Therefore adult education will have to concentrate upon the abolition of discrimination and prejudice, especially with regard to the second generation.

Thinking of 'the challenges of the 1990s' I would like to make a double final statement. Adult education has to direct itself at specific groups and problem areas. Such a task lies beyond reform euphoria or disenchantment. But the orientation at specific target groups must not lead to a fractioning or segmentation of society whereby adult education would only address deficit-groups. Then, adult education would become a kind of fire-department, which fights the flames it has itself been kindling (KNOLL, 1982). Adult education has also to fulfil a general social task, it has to contribute to the behavioural qualification which all adults will need for the 'Third Industrial Revolution'. Multicultural education is an essential part of this kind of future new behaviour.

Secondly : the opening paper by W. Leirman, "Adult Education : Movement and Discipline between the Golden Sixties and the Iron Eighties" does not, to me, cause any kind of resignation as to the future of our science. There are quite some educational challenges, and realism is certainly not the worst virtue !

NOTES

(1) This is especially the case with the German groups in the U.S.A..
(2) An announced special issue of Bildung und Erziehung, edited by W. Mitter, and devoted to integration, to appear in 1987, will deserve our special attention.
(3) In view of its complexity, we do not deal here with the issue of integration of German Jews.
(4) In the FRG, 'seed-money' was offered for the return of Turkish immigrants to their homeland. Up to now 70,000 people have applied. It is impossible to assess the cultural and linguistic effects of such measures.
(5) In Canada, citizenship is awarded three years after (legitimate) immigration, through a rather formal jurisdictional act. In the FRG, citizenship for immigrants is tied in with a complex procedure which sometimes touches on the grotesque.

REFERENCES

Anweiler, D. and Kuebart, F. (1985) 'Internacional-'noe vospitanie' und 'multicultural education' in, Wie Vor, Bd. I, 219
Dahm, G. et al. (eds) (1980) Wörterbuch der Weiterbildung, München
Daudlin, B. (ed.) (1984) Equality now. Report of the Special Committee on Visible Minorities in Canada's society, Canada House of Commons, Ottowa
Gerbaulet, S. (1986) 'Kirchen, Kultusminister, Koranschulen, Kaum Religionsunterricht für Türken', Die Zeit, nr. 16, 61
Knoll, J.H. et al. (1984) Automatenspiel und Freizeitverhalten Jugendlichen. Eine Untersuchung zur pädagogischen Problematik von Video-Automaten, Grafenan
Knoll, J.H. (1985) 'Erwachsenenbildung nur lokale Feuer-wehr?' In wieweit kann Weiterbildung

Zielgruppenarbeit leisten?', Volkshochschule im Westen, 34, 347 s

Knoll, J.H., Kolfhaus, S., Pfeifer, S. and Swoboda, W. (1986) Das Bildschirmspiel in pädagogischer Forschung und im Alltag Jugendlicher, Leverkusen

Knoll, J.H. (1986) Multikulturelle Bildung in Schule und Erwachsenenbildung - als Beispiel : das Bildungswesen der dänischen Minderheit in Südschleswig in A. Benning (ed.), Erwachsenenbildung - Bilanz und Zukunftsperspektiven, Schöningh, Paderborn

Knoll, J.H. (1987) 'Multikulturalismus, multikulturelle Bildung und Erwachsenenbildung in Kanada - von aussen gesehen' in, Internationales Jahrbuch der Erwachsenenbildung, Köln/Wien (to be published)

Mallea, J.R. and Shea, E.C. (1979) Multiculturalism and Education, a select bibliography, The Ontario Institute for Studies in Education, Toronto

Mitter, W. and Swift, J. (eds.) (1985) 'Erziehung und die Vielfalt der Kulturen. Der Beitrag der vergleichenden Erziehungswissenschaft' in, Bildung und Erziehung, Beiheft 2/1, Köln/Wien

Roosens, E. Ethnic groups and ethnic identity, Symbols or concepts, Fac. Psych. and Ed. Sc., n.d., Leuven (manuscript)

Roosens, E. (1985) The social-cultural Structure (Kroeber Lecture), Univ. of California, Berkeley

Roosens E. The structure of an ethnic consciousness, Leuven Univ. Press, Bd., Leuven

Siebert, H. (ed.) (1979) Taschenbuch der Weiterbildung, Baltmannsweiler

Silbermann, A. and Schoeps, B. (1986) Antisemitismus nach dem Holocaust, Köln

----- Start here, Ethnic Groups in Canada, UBC Library, no. 118, Vancouver

Tsivion, A., Tokatli, R., Laufert, L. and Grebelsky, O. (1983) 'The Tehila Project' in, Adult Basic Education (Report of the Conference in St. Andrews, Scotland, Europ. Bur. of Ad. Ed.), Amersfoort

Unesco (1985) 4th World Conference on Adult education. Final report, Paris

Vath, R. (1984) 'Professionalisierung in der Erwachsenenbildung' in, Enzyklopädie Erziehungswissenschaft, Bd. 11, Erwachsenenbildung (ed. by E. Schnitz and A. Tietgens), Stuttgart

Wirth, I. (ed.) (1978) <u>Handwörterbuch der Erwachsenenbildung</u>, Schöningh, Paderborn

Chapter Ten
THE MORAL BASE OF DEVELOPMENT

Louis BAECK
Cath. University of Leuven
Belgium

1. The postwar period in a nutshell

We first want to present an overview of the major evolutions in terms of East-West and North-South relations since 1945.

The East-West conflict

The end of the Second World War caused a breach in the power relations at the world level. The Western European nations, on whose behalf it had all started, had dealt themselves a severe blow. Most of them have as a consequence lost their international influence and power. A new era started, whereby two non-European colossi remained as superpowers, namely the United States and the Soviet Union. Western Europe emerged totally weakened from that battle. It became a member of the Atlantic Alliance, which would, under the direction of the United States, operate as one Western block in the postwar period. Japan would become member too in the 1960s.

The new development model which the United States presented to the postwar Western World, was a mixture of Rooseveltian idealism and of pragmatism, inspired by the self-interest of the victorious superpower. In the planetary vision of the United States the following action points occupied a central place :

1. Regulation of international disputes through a multilateral political consultation body, the United Nations.
2. Development of an economic space inspired by supranational principles, the famous 'open-door policy', concretely realized by GATT

and OESO.
3. A defense system (NATO) which would serve for the proper sphere of influence as a shield against external and internal aggression.
4. Phasing out of colonial dependencies on the basis of the right to self-determination of people. Up to now the colonial ties were notably favourable to European nations (Great-Britain, France, Belgium, Portugal, Spain) and this imperial preference was a thorn in the side of the United States.

For Europe and Japan, the first task was reconstruction of their economy and their society. For this goal, the United States have offered considerable support. The reconstruction of Europe and Japan evolved quickly and it can figure as a success story. At this moment the central nations of the European Community (France, Germany, the Benelux countries) have reached the same level of average productivity and income as the United States. And Japan is not lagging far behind. At the economic level, the hegemonic position of the United States is no longer what it used to be. The postwar supranational order has therefore been weakened and in some areas, the United States, Europe and Japan are in some areas one another's rival.

The North-South tension

Few events will have had such a profound influence on our time and still keep that influence as the quickly succeeding decolonization waves in Asia, in the Middle East and in Africa. At the same time the nations of Latin America started to show a more assertive attitude after 1945.

The emancipation of the colonies was quickened in a large degree by the postwar world system. The two superpowers were involved in the cold war, and they thought that after the colonial powers had left a vacuum, they could considerably enlarge their sphere of influence by entering it.

On the other hand the United Nations, which had been blocked in their peace mission by the cold war, took up the role of herald of the development-idea for the so-called 'Third World'. By means of their Social Economic Council and of their specialized bodies (Unesco, FAO, WHO, PNUD, later UNCTAD and UNIDO) the United Nations would take the role of teacher and guide in the area of development. During the years 1950-60 the idea of development was spread on a planetary base.

On the side of the Western nations, the policy of the United States as a hegemonic leader was predominant. Its policy was streamlined along the following lines of action :

1. Establishment of governments of befriended leaders; and if possible, also a government which would earn the support of large parts of public opinion.
2. Development of a mass-consumption economy : first for the urban elites, and later for broader segments of the population.
3. Transplantation of Western, and preferably American organization-patterns for these young nations in development.
4. Military and financial support in the struggle against internal and external (communist) subversion.

This optimistic vision reached its peak with the announcement of the 'Alliance for Progress' by President J.F. Kennedy.

Since the beginning of the 1960s the all too rapid 'westernization' caused problems and tensions in the Third World. Here and there radical opposition movements emerged (in Latin America, in South East Asia, in Africa) and in many Third World countries the military took over the power from the civilian leaders. They were supported by the West as a stabilization factor, i.e. as a dam against undesirable radicalization. The idea of development and especially of development cooperation lost much of its original spell on account of these changes.

During the 1970s the governments of the developing countries launched a diplomatic offensive through the channel of United Nations organizations known under the name 'New International Economic Order'. In the West, these initiatives received little or no support. And even in the developing world, reform of the economic world order did not really get a firm footing. It soon appeared that the N.I.E.O. would especially benefit a small group (i.e. the elite) and that the basic development of aspirations of the masses would be overlooked. China, the biggest developing country, did not cooperate. And only the oil sheiks profited by the idea, by the implementation of administered oil-prices. After the failure of N.I.E.O., some UN organizations have switched to the idea of basic needs. But in official circles of the developing countries, the model of basic needs finds only a few enthusiastic followers. This idea manifests itself mainly in the new socio-cultural 'grass roots movements' who inspired themselves on the basis of ethical principles for development.

The elites of developing countries on the other hand have in many cases chosen a path of development which has led to the following general pattern :

1. hasty westernization of the urban centres;
2. unequal social and geographical distribution of the fruits of development;
3. frustration of the masses;
4. exorbitant financial debt to foreign countries, followed by financial control of the IMF over their economic policies.

Since about the middle of the 1970s we have seen the springing up of 'grass roots movements' inspired by religious and/or ethical principles : the fundamentalists in the Islamic world, the reform movements in Brazil and in the Philippines and elsewhere. They react against the authoritarian course of the military leaders, etc. The failure of modernizing elites left a vacuum that has been filled up by the so-called 'moral base'. We can also notice a similar shift on a more theoretical level, e.g. in the theories of development. This new social-cultural matrix offers new perspectives for theory as well as for practice.

2. The crisis in development theory

The mainstream version of the period 1950-65
Decolonization meant a challenge to the intellectual circles of the West. The question was : according to which guide-lines could the new countries, called developing countries, organize their 'take off' ? This question caused an intense theoretical activity in the 'think tanks' and in the universities of Europe and the United States. In the stream of publications a development theory evolved which, because of its dominance, was called 'mainstream version'.

This theory showed much resemblance to socio-economic publications at the end of the 19th and the beginning of the 20th century, when traditional ideas and institutions of Western Europe underwent a strong erosion under the influence of modernization, industrialization and urbanization. A reformulation of the theories of Spencer, Durkheim and Weber, with an eye on the developing countries, was worked out especially in North American universities. Here, the development scenarios for the Third World were perceived as a repetition of the Western developmental path. In the same vein its economic version proposed the West as a model for the Third World (1).

The main points of the mainstream version are the following :

1. secularization of vision of man and society as well as of the organization of society;
2. modernization of society through the devaluation of its own past, e.g. of its own tradition :
   - a take-over of modern (Western) behaviour patterns; education would have to play the role of a lever;
   - urbanization as the global path towards modernization;
   - adoption of 'cosmopolitan attitudes' supported by the culture-industry (press, television and other mass media systems);
3. economic growth by promoting <u>industrialization</u> and by a relative neglect of agriculture, this being too traditional a sector;
4. at the political level, the model opted for 'nation building' by taking over Western political blue prints.

A minority of historians, anthropologists, philosophers, and even economists, criticized the mainstream version. In their criticism they stated that the 'mainstream version' was not concerned with the authentic development of the Third World but focused too exclusively on 'westernization'. They also stated that the elite-absorption model left the masses out there in the cold. A critical understream of theoreticians thought that this model of development would sooner or later provoke protest movements. The failure of the first generation of political leaders in their quest for rapid modernization and the fact that they were often replaced by military juntas, taking up the task of curbing this protest, justifies their criticism.

The 'dependencia' school

Under the direction of R. Prebisch in Latin America, a group of sociologists and economists was formed within the regional UN-organization. This group did not perceive underdevelopment as a consequence of tradition, or of a failure of educated labour forces, of a lack of capital, etc. but as a consequence of the too great dependency (dependencia) on the West. Underdevelopment was no longer seen as a shortcoming in modernization on the side of developing nations, but as a consequence of Western penetration and of dominance, first of a colonial and later of a post-colonial nature. The radical dependencia school offered as a solution the delinking of the international relationships and ties with the outside world, in order to promote national and authentic development.

During the 1970s the dependencia school of thought underwent a radicalization through the adoption of the Marxist paradigm of unequal change and exploitation. According to this tendency, true development was to be pursued through a switch of the Third World to the socialist model. Some developing countries (Angola, Ethiopia, Afghanistan, etc.) followed that road, but they lapsed into a still more visible dependencia towards the Soviet Union.

The search for authentic development

Since the end of the 1970s, the crisis mentality prevails in the theoretical circles who are dealing with development problems. In a provocative essay, the famous developmental economist A. Hirschman states that "much of the zest and hope that characterized work in this area of economics in the 1950s and 1960s is no longer present" (HIRSCHMAN, 1982). In a recent study the economist H. Bruton (BRUTON, 1985, p. 286) further develops this idea. Bruton used to be one of the well-known exponents of the 'mainstream development theory' and is now engaging in self-criticism. We quote him :

> With only limited exceptions, in both the literature and in practice, development has come to mean a replication of the West ... the equalization of development with westernization impeded the construction of an authentic development theory (BRUTON, 1985, p. 286).

The Moral Base of Development

Well-known students of economic development admit now the failure of theory and of practice according to the mainstream theory. This failure is the consequence of an inadequate paradigm : development was seen as displacement of the traditional system by a modern (Western) system at great social economic and cultural costs.

Sociologists and anthropologists also engaged in a critical interrogation of mainstream thinking from 1950 to about 1970 and they stress "the loss of cultural identity" under the influence of "westernization". And since the fundamentalist renaissance in the Middle East, the secularization thesis of the mainstream theory has also come under heavy attack. The take-over of Iran by the Shiah clergy has also put the moral base in development dynamics into sharper focus (see e.g. BENARD and KHALILZAD, 1984).

But not only practitioners and theoreticians of the West, but also those who adhere to radical socialist models are confronted with grass roots protest. After the radical approach of Mao Zedong, China has now reverted to a more flexible policy. It is one where capitalistic impulses are brought into the social-economic system. And at the international level, one notices a prudent opening towards the West. This radical change is clearly the consequence of social pressure from the masses against a too authoritarian policy. Yet also in other parts of the world, the socialist development model does not seem to be a magic formula. In Afghanistan the resistance against this model is visible to everbody.

The socialist development theories do not know how to handle 'displaced peasants, urban slum dwellers, ethnic minorities, etc.' For they do not fit into the dual class model of capitalist versus proletarian. We can consider these masses as marginalized, but not as 'proletarians' with a revolutionary conscience.

The moral base
I am of the opinion that the crisis in practice and in theory is largely due to the neglect of the moral base :

1. In the West, development was identified with 'westernization'; and the other superpower put development on a level with 'sovietization'.

The Moral Base of Development

2. The one-sided modernization and industrialization thesis has implanted costly enclaves of modernism with neglect of the traditional sectors.
3. The secularization thesis made the mistake of taking the European modernization of the 18th and the 19th centuries as a model. The resistance of the traditional culture and especially of the indigenous religion in many developing countries has proved to be tougher than expected. The same factor equally plays a role behind the iron curtain, as is witnessed by Poland.
4. The authoritarian development models provoke sooner or later a resistance from the masses, so that the military authorities either restrain themselves or are replaced, as e.g. in Brazil, Uruguay, Argentina, the Philippines, etc.

The new socio-cultural movements propelled by the moral base adhere to a development strategy that, in the specialized literature, is known under the name of basic-needs model.

In contrast to the mainstream model with its unspecified but built in preference for the development of elites, the basic-needs model resolutely focuses on target groups in the population by stressing the struggle against poverty and by giving priority to projects that promote employment. Considering the bleak misery and massive unemployment that prevail in many parts of the world, this seems to be a salutary correction to the conventional perception of development policy.

Specifically, the basic-needs model stresses the following :

1. Employment opportunities of the poorest groups must be expanded in order to increase their income.
2. To improve the employment situation, more investments must be made in the sectors that have been neglected, i.e. among the rural masses and in the informal urban sector.
3. Fundamental services such as education, health care, and public transport must be made more available to these neglected sectors.
4. Institutions that stimulate the participation of the people as a whole must be

5. On the institutional and material level, more reliance must be placed on the means available in the village itself. Where possible, self-reliance must be stressed.

The models that give precedence to basic needs and advocate growth with less one sided distribution have been supported in the international forum by the International Labour Organization and the World Bank. But most policy-making circles in the First World and, naturally, the privileged groups of the Third World countries support a national growth pattern, because the basic-needs model presumes rather drastic social and political reforms.

3. The moral base at work

In Latin America the moral base has been in operation for two decades already. It manifests itself by means of numerous religiously inspired basic communities : the so-called <u>basista</u> movement (Movimientos de Base). In this respect especially socially moved pastors have played for years the role of change agent. After the second Vatican council, the initially regime-bound Church has taken a more free position with regard to the state machine and to the established power groups. After an intensive ideological struggle between conservatives and future oriented elements within itself, the Church has opted for the emancipation of the deprived groups in society.

1. Through a more socially oriented gospel-preaching against oppression and injustice. Since the 1970s, the Church has been a defender of human rights in authoritarian regimes in Latin-America.
2. Liberation theology functions as ideology of emancipation against internal as well as external manipulation.
   - On the one hand liberation theology strives at 'delinking' from intellectual paternalism, which is exerted by Western European and North American theology. Liberation theologians think that the secularizing-theology of Western Europe and of Northern America is inadequate, when one looks at the historical and cultural aspirations of the Latin-American societies. They perceive

Western theology as too rationalistic and too alienated from the people. They thus throw a dam against imported models.
- But also internally, the basista groups take an anti-elitist position. They work with small, limited units which are independent of large organizations such as parties, labour unions, and other big organizations. They direct their action at 'conscientization' with local, limited objectives. The 'conventional wisdom' of (official) expert 'outsiders' such as economists, sociologists and also educationists is taken with a great dose of scepticism. The main orientation is 'self-reliance'.

It is clear that this way of working in the profound layers of society has a positive effect. The question is whether this kind of in-depth operation can be sufficiently effective in its actual (dualistic) isolation. The prime movers of complex societies are and remain big organizational units such as parties, labour unions and other well structured organizations. The basic communities can work as a ferment among the deep layers of society. But if they want to get beyond mere 'conscientization' and become operational, a mass organization with inevitable bureaucratic techniques is indispensable. For, to say it in metaphorical language : "small is beautiful, big is powerful, but only the combination of the two is successful".

As an economist, I cannot offer a ready-made solution for the problem of this 'combination'. But I may hope that in this conference of adult educators, workable formulas can be found towards such a combination.

NOTES

(1) See e.g. the 'Theory of the five stages' of W. Rostow, where the developing nations are invited to organize their 'take off' according to the five phases that developed (Western) nations have gone through.

REFERENCES

Benard, Ch. and Khalilzad, Z. (1984) *The Government of God*, New York
Bruton, H. (1985) 'The Search for a Development Economics' in, *World Development*, n°10
Hirschman, A. (1982) 'The Rise and Decline of Development Economics' in M. Gersovitz (ed.), *The theory and Experience of Economic Development*, London

Chapter Eleven
DIALOGUE TOWARDS DEVELOPMENT AND THE DEVELOPMENT OF DIALOGUE

Antonio Faundez
World Council of Churches
Geneva, Switzerland

Education and dialogue
We will develop some ideas about what we call essential evidences. This will necessarily confront us with the negation of these ideas. In other words we want to analyze those things which in a historical perspective have become - or have been imposed as - obvious. We will try to show that throughout history many non-essentials have organized our lives as substitutes of what is really essential.

If we analyze the French verb which indicates the action of knowing - nl. con-naître - and the learning of the process that leads to the appropriation of knowledge, we clearly see that participation is a substantial part of that process. Indeed, the verb 'con-naître' has two parts. One part indicates a common birth. The other part indicates a 'cohabitation', thus to be born together, to live with something or somebody. Thus, the action of knowing, the process of learning is a shared activity which gives birth to two human beings participating in the confinement which makes them learn.

What we want to underline is, first of all the fact that though participation of the individual is fundamental and indispensable, the process of developing knowledge is a social process. Further, the process also implies by necessity the interaction of at least two human beings, and the action of knowing gives them a common birth. We would like to add a third characteristic which we also think to be essential. We would like to talk about an implicit aspect in the action of knowing, in the process of being born together. We mean the action of rebirth, because we consider this shared action as a permanent 'renaissance' or renewal both for the participants and for knowledge itself. Thus understanding is being reborn each and every moment, all along the process of creation of knowledge. The 'renaissance' is permanent. This makes us aware of the fact that each and every educational process has to be a permanent creation.

It is important to refuse those models which pretend to be universal in the field of education. One of the most frequent mistakes is the application of educational models for each and every reality, which are considered as unique and uniform, as if only one reality exists. Such a uniformization neglects, consciously or unconsciously, the evident diversity of reality by imposing a univocal model on a reality which could be quite different. Given a multiformal reality (every one with specific characteristics) we have to avoid in education and development, reference to those models. Later on, we will come back to this subject. Just as each reality is different, the educational process has also to be different, but not in the sense that it is an imitation of a corresponding educational process from another reality. Because the activities concerning education and development are particular to every society, there exists a great diversity. Therefore one can hardly speak about "models" in this sense. Thus there is no satisfactory model, and accepting one would certainly betray the real process of knowledge. Nevertheless the general trend consists of establishing fixed models and methods. The method, however, is a track, a road which leads to some result. It consists of theoretical and practical principles which are simply a leading thread. These principles must be constantly created in different political and social situations, even if these situations have certain things in common. A method must never be considered as a fixed model. The process of knowledge and education is not a process of imitation but on the contrary a process of creation.

The process of knowledge does not only appear at the level of words, although people often understand it in this way. Nor does it concern a simple theory based on language. The action of knowledge acquires a larger dimension across every daily practice. Every action, situated at any level, be it economical, familial, political, or ontological, has been replaced by a counter-evidence : the separation of theory and practice. Clearly every process of knowledge is at the same time theoretical and practical. This relationship is dialectical, which means that both aspects are permanently intertwined.

All essential evidences are undoubtedly historical. This means they are objects of historical development. Thus, they are not static either in quantity or in content; they do not constitute a whole unchangeable or eternal dogmas. Every historical moment and every social reality "reads" in a specific and different manner the evidences and counter-evidences. This is the reason why it is impossible to determine once and for all a defined number of essential evidences or counter-evidences. We only try to propose some by reconsidering the long and critical tradition of some theorists of education who not only emphasise the positive characteristics of the process of knowledge, but most of all expose the negative characteristics of the counter-evidences. In this way they have opposed the social essential of the act of "knowing" to the individual contra-essential; the essential of the "common birth" to the contra-essential of a hierarchy of knowledge; the essential of creating the act of knowing to the process of imitation; a multiple and diversified essential of knowledge to the uniformity of process, etc. ... We do not pretend to present here an exhaustive list of those evidences or counter-evidences nor do we pretend to give an exhaustive analysis of these contradictions. Other theorists have already for a long time been elucidating these themes, and they have in their practice as in their theory, unveiled and deepened the political role of the evidences and counter-evidences in education.

The analysis of the essential evidences and the so-called counter-evidences which pretend to be substitutes forces us to deal with some fundamental questions. How can the historical emergence of these counter-evidences be explained? What are the mechanisms which bring about the negation of the essential evidences of the knowledge process? How can we explain the fact that the action of knowing (in the sense of a common birth or a 'renaissance') is in opposition with the action of teaching which includes a relationship between a dominant subject and a dominated object? How to explain, in relation to the essential evidence that knowledge is of a social nature, the counter-evidence that this process is strictly individual? How to explain, in relation to the fact that knowledge is essentially both theoretical and practical - which means that there are two aspects of one global phenomenon, the opinion that theoretical knowledge is different from practical knowledge, and that both are independent of one another? How to explain that the process of knowledge, which certainly is a process of permanent creation, is in conflict with the chain of imitation models applied in any kind of context? How to explain that the evidence of the essential diversity, the diversity of reality, stands against the concept of a uniform reality?

Certainly the reasons are both historical and political. The process of knowledge is a concrete historical reality, which is marked and determined by it. One of the essential characteristics of the historical and social reality is the existence of dominant and dominated groups, dominant and dominated nations. This domination is not only manifest on the social level, but also on the individual one. The fact that certain social groups dominate other groups, certain individuals dominate other individuals, certain countries dominate others, is related to the question of power. Domination consists in the exercising of power upon somebody or upon some community. Human history cannot be explained without putting the question of power. Thus, given the fact that the action of knowing is both social and historical, it also reveals the problem of power. It is in this perspective that we have to try and find an explanation for the birth of the relationship between knowledge and power. Further we think that the replacement of the essential evidences by opposite ones can be situated precisely in this political aspect of the social and historical reality, which consists in exercising domination upon some human beings or social groups. If we want to re-discover the essential evidences of the action of knowledge, we have to overcome this historical holy union between knowledge and power. The reason is that as long as certain social groups will dominate others, the identification of knowledge with power will survive. Re-discovery of essential evidences of "knowing" and "learning" is above all struggle against the traditional power concept in society. We think that the action of education is closely connected to that of knowing and that education acquires its characteristic dimension of action and political struggle in the historical context. The action of knowing, the action of educating is political, because they are realized in a context of social domination, where power is exercised by some human beings or social groups over other human beings or social groups.

When we consider the plain but also complex truth of power in society, we can better understand its mechanism. In a determined society, without any doubt, the dominant groups distribute power among the different social strata. These are charged with different activities, especially determined to reproduce the social relations of that specific society. Thus, individuals or groups responsible for the educational process, only receive a minor part of the power (connected with knowledge) in order to reproduce, through education, the ideology that guarantees their power and also the necessary practice to maintain that society.

Because the action of knowing, of renaissance, of education and self-education takes place in a highly hierarchical society, groups which possess power, for the same reason possess the knowledge. This means that these groups are the ones which determine what "knowledge" should be, with the intention to reproduce their power. The same groups offer some of the crumbs of their power to the "responsibles" charged with "conducting" the process of knowledge. In doing so they interrelate their knowledge and their power and present it as universal. It is true that each social or individual relation is in every possible way a power relation. Nevertheless this power becomes manifest in different ways. The power that we are going to analyze is directly linked to our thoughts, to our work, although it is not distinct from the political and economical power. The necessity to transform and to create a new type of relation between the participants of the educational process, certainly supposes the creation of new power relations between the participants of the general socio-political process. And, just as it is the case on the cultural level, or on the level of knowledge, the relations mostly become manifest through authoritarianism. A society structured into dominating groups and groups which are supposed to accept that power, has structured any social phenomenon in the same way. Indeed the political structure of the society defines the quantity of power available for those who possess the culture and the knowledge. The dominating social classes give those concepts a specific kind of significance. The determination of the content of culture and knowledge is simply based on the power of the dominating classes. In general the intellectuals and especially the teachers or "the experts", are forced to reproduce a certain type of social relation in order to execute their tasks. It is a fact that in every society, even in the strongest and the most close ones, there exist degrees of liberty, which make it possible to propose solutions to change that kind of power relation. But those alternatives have a very weak position compared to the dominating and ideological forces and, consequently compared to the strata which possess political-economical power in the society. It must be clear that a new concept of the process of knowledge can only be based on the notion of participation. When we are talking about participation, we do not refer to a passive kind of participation that is only partially exercised in certain sectors of the educational or social process. On the contrary, we are referring to an active participation at any moment and in any field. The acquisition of the participatory capacity is an essential task to every participant of the educational process.

The only way to create some knowledge and to create oneself, consists in knowing how to learn from the other, by renouncing the traditional conceptions associated with power and knowledge. It is only in this perspective, in which the teacher also is pupil and master, artist and administrator, that he will be a participant in the political process. It is only in this way that the social task can be accomplished and can take an active part in the social life in order to elaborate a more democratic society, with more freedom, more equality and more solidarity.

To give the process of knowledge its real meaning, its essential evidence, we think it is necessary to take into account the political dimension and furthermore to act consistently.

It is certain that the action which fosters knowledge contains a struggle on the political level in order to succeed in re-creating the essential dialogue between the participants of the exchange. Knowing further means the struggle for the creating of a real method of knowing, which makes possible the renaissance of the participants. It is necessary, if we want this operation to be successful, to recreate a new practice of power, a new conception of power and also to re-create society by the practice of freedom and democracy because this gives back the real meaning to the act of knowing in its true sense, that is to say sociability, humanity and solidarity.

One of the frequent mistakes in the domain of the creation of knowledge and education consists in the confusing of the transmission of information and knowledge with the act of education. In our opinion education is above all a process of learning through permanent dialogue. Learning also includes teaching which above all means learning to put questions and to discover those which are essential to the participation of beings (individuals or collectivities). However, learning to put essential questions also necessitates the discovery of the constituting elements of the fundamental questions. These activities are difficult, both intellectually and practically, but they are fundamentally pedagogical. In <u>Towards an Education of Questions</u>, written in Spanish by Paolo Freire and myself, we represent this new type of education. We try to indicate how the system and the methodology in the field of education is in general characterized by a process of answering questions, that indeed never have been put by most of the participants. What matters here is the mastering of a methodology characterized by a critical and creative dimension, where the questions and answers are probably temporary but at the same time essential.

The very old and new way of understanding, the act of knowing shows us to what extent participation, as we have already seen, is fundamental. If we examine the actual educational process, we must admit that participation, in most of the cases, fails in a pitiful way. Thus, certain elements which are in most cases considered as relevant to the responsibility of the "master" or the "expert" are also part of the responsibility of the "pupil". If the educational process must bring answers to the fundamental questions of all participants, they themselves will have to distinguish the essential questions which need an answer. Therefore the programming of the process, the preparation of the necessary didactical material or the permanent evaluation activities are an essential part of the act of learning. Thus a true educational process includes the allowance of the active participation of all participants, in every stage of the process, whether it concerns the preparation of the material or the organization, and the participation, to an ongoing criticizing of the process itself.

Education for development and the development of education

These ideas which we want to elaborate now have no universal character. They are the product of our multiple experiences with communities in several African and Latin American areas, where we have definitely learned more than we have taught. For this reason we do not want to propose a model here, but rather a temporary reflection. Indeed, there exist in Europe and elsewhere, other interesting actual experiences, new practices and reflections in the field of education and development which are promising approaches. The truth only becomes manifest through dialogue, through an exchange of our particular insights and our different experiences. Therefore we think that such an exchange will contribute to a large extent to more democratic and solidary solutions for a number of fundamental problems, including some important questions in the field of education and development.

The theses we have developed above can be adapted to the whole of the process itself. Indeed we consider the development as if it were an educational process regarding all people of a community. To consider development as a process of education also means that education should be considered as a process of development, as they are inseparable. This is the reason why education for development also implies the development of education. But such a conception supposes a different interpretation of the two concepts. Earlier we have declared that our concept is related to the act of knowing, to the act of learning, to a process including how to learn, to dialogue. We will now try to develop some thoughts about the concept of development. Such a concept cannot be defined, unless it is in accordance with needs of the people. Thus it acquires a new dimension, because this does not simply refer to the needs of the economic order. The criticisms about theory and practice of development in the 1960s and the 1970s did not question the essential errors. One of the fundamental errors consists in, in our view, that in theory and practice of development only the economic aspect is taken into consideration. In our opinion, the supporters of this conception forgot - consciously or unconsciously - that in any case economics cannot be separated from politics, neither can other areas in life and society. In a new concept the political or educational and cultural dimension should be taken into consideration. This concept of development touches the problem of participation. Because, when development is known as a way to solve the needs of the community, above all it is necessary to define those needs. This task necessarily implies the active participation of the whole community, which must discover itself the proper needs. This kind of action is very educational, touching directly popular education which aims at improving the local life of the majorities. This aspect of development until now has been systematically neglected. The projects or the programmes that were carried out, were a matter for "experts" who have determined the important questions in a somewhat arbitrary way. The same thing happened to needs of a society, a nation, a community and even a total continent.

In the given society, the needs arise as a result of political and economical struggles. It appears to be necessary to make a distinction between what we can call the expressed needs and the real needs. One of the essential objectives of a critical analysis of reality precisely consists in determining the important question and real needs. Most of the expressed needs in our society are in fact the result of the situation in which the production is even more conceived for profit making rather than for the expression of real needs.

The people in general escape from the cultural penetration, from live-models, from artificial needs that do not correspond to their real problems. And, this penetration is accomplished at the present moment with the help of an impressive chain of communication possibilities which support the economical and political power structures. This ideological apparatus diffuses a society model, which is undoubtedly essential for its own reproduction, but it does not necessarily correspond to the real needs of a given society.

The discovery of the real needs of the majorities is a difficult and complex process, because there does not exist, as it happens, any educational model, and economical model, which can be proposed to the communities to discover their own needs. There only exist theoretical and practical principles. We have discussed some of them in this paper. It seems unnecessary to emphasize the fact that these principles must be adapted and applied in a creative way to each social and historical situation. Birth in a country, a village, does not necessarily guarantee the knowledge of that country or village. The knowledge of it supposes an intellectual and practical effort. The abstraction enables the penetration into the concrete and vice versa; it also enables the understanding and transformation of reality. It is the people's task to participate in this initiative. They already have practical knowledge of their own reality, they undergo it, but most of the time without a real comprehension of what is happening. It is necessary in this stage to pass from "doxa" to "epistême" and from "opinion" to "comprehension" through dialogue and through a theoretical and practical process. The "feeling" of the people is already in itself an empirical knowledge which enables them to solve a number of problems. They create in this way a certain number of techniques, of practices, of ideas that makes it possible to master reality. This knowledge acquired in close contact with reality is certainly indispensable in the elaboration and the application of every development programme.

In general, the programmes are a means to transfer scientific knowledge which is considered as superior to the people. Every other type of knowledge is then considered as inferior or simply as a negation of knowledge. This kind of problem concerns without any doubt the programmes which are related to education and development, but also to the formation (education) of animators or technicians. As far as the animation of the people is concerned, it is on the contrary necessary to promote a dialogue between popular knowledge and scientific knowledge. This is not an easy task. The past and the present stimulate the over-estimation of scientific knowledge related to nature and society and the under-estimation of 'popular knowledge'.

The transfer of scientific knowledge needs a permanent dialogue with the people. The technicians and animators must understand that, without the participation of the people, the application of the "knowledge" will have no effect. They also have to understand that it is meanwhile essential that this transfer takes place, because it enables the people to strengthen their real force and to acquire more independence day by day. The only way to accomplish this social task that rests on their shoulders, to contribute effectively to the creation of a different society, consists in learning with the people. They have to find out which kind of "feeling" the people have, what is their empirical knowledge, so as to make the scientific knowledge they already have more lively. In this way the people are able to appropriate this scientific knowledge and intregrate it within the empirical knowledge they have already mastered. This enables them to create a new type of knowledge, that helps them to understand reality in order to transform it.

Here we see that the education for development must force itself to detect the real needs of society and has to search for the real solution among all solutions that society can offer. This is to happen both in traditional and the modern sector. When we speak about all of resources, we do not only refer to resources in the material or technical sense, but we also think about other types of resources, especially the ones that emerge from social, cultural and political organizations.

Every development programme must take into consideration the active participation of the entire people. Without this cooperation the programme will be a farce, an 'affair' for experts. It will certainly fail if it does not come to terms with the real needs of the communities. Such a failure will necessarily reproduce the model of an unjust society. Only an active and critical participation of the people in the entire educational and developmental programme guarantees successful results.

Chapter Twelve
THE UNIVERSITY AND ADULT EDUCATION : THE NEWEST ROLE
AND RESPONSIBILITY OF THE UNIVERSITY

Jindra KULICH
University of British Columbia
Vancouver, Canada

Throughout the history of mankind, bands, tribes, societies and nations depended on the ability of their members to learn and to change. Social, spiritual, political, intellectual, cultural and technical development depended on this ability, as did the quality of life and indeed ultimately the survival of the individuals and of their society.
With the growing complexity of society and the challenges facing it, more and more of the learning required occurred in formal educational settings. Universal public education of the young became the panacea in recent history. In the second half of the twentieth century we have come to realize that schooling of children and youth no longer is sufficient, and that learning is a lifelong process which needs to be supported by broadly conceived and based lifelong education provision.
In his opening paper, Walter Leirman provided us with a concise and yet broad context in which society, we as individuals, and adult education existed and developed in the last twenty years. My paper, dealing with the newest role and responsibility of the university in lifelong education is set against that background.

Definitions
I need to make a key distinction at the outset. It is a distinction which is not always made in the recent proliferation of writing on lifelong learning. It is a distinction between learning and education. Learning is a natural process which occurs throughout life and which most of the time is incidental, unplanned, left to chance. Education is a conscious, planned, systematic and sequential process, based on

defined learning objectives and using specific learning procedures ; such objectives and procedures are designed by an external agent (such as an institution or a teacher) in a mutual agreement between the agent and the learner, or by the learner himself. Learning can and does occur in the natural societal setting, but it is enhanced in more formal instructional setting where the element of chance is minimized (VERNER and BOOTH, 1964 ; CROPLEY, 1979).

The other, and perhaps even more important, conceptual clarification needs to be made regarding lifelong education. Again, there is a veritable explosion of writing about lifelong education, continuous education, continuing education and adult continuing education. These terms are often used interchangeably, or different meaning is attached to the same term by different writers. This babel is perhaps most marked in English-language literature. Some adult educators have gone as far as to make lifelong education synonymous with adult education, thus claiming the term for themselves and pre-empting other component parts of the lifelong education provision.

Paul Lengrand, one of the foremost exponents of the concept of lifelong education, provides us with the original definition (italics are mine) :

> What we mean by lifelong education is a series of very specific ideas, experiments and achievements, in other words, education in the full sense of the word, including all its aspects and dimensions, <u>its uninterrupted development from the first moments of life to the very last</u> and the close, organic interrelationship between the various points and successive phases in its development... It will be seen that the concept of lifelong education is circular : there can only be lifelong education worthy of the name if people receive in childhood a fair and rational education... but an education of this kind (that is lifelong education) cannot be achieved unless adult education itself is firmly established in people's minds and way of life... (LENGRAND, 1975).

Thus it is clear that adult (or if you wish, continuing) education is an important <u>part</u> of lifelong education, but it cannot lay claim to <u>being</u> lifelong education.

By now it will be obvious that I am willing to

accept adult education and continuing education as being synonymous, a practice widespread in North America. I do not see the need for the term adult continuing education, since I do not accept that lifelong education and continuing education are synonymous.

University extension

It is evident that the university (and here and throughout this paper I will be using this term to cover all types of higher education institutions) is only one among the many institutions responsible for the provision of continuing education, but it plays a crucial role in this respect for a significant segment of society. The university has an acknowledged unique role in generating new knowledge and in research. It also provides an important part of the comprehensive provision of lifelong education, both through its undergraduate and graduate teaching and its continuing education programs. From their beginning the universities have been contributing to the provision of lifelong education and learning. Their most significant, and for most of their history their only, contribution was the teaching of full-time undergraduate and graduate students. Their contribution to continuing education, the university extension idea, first originated at the Cambridge University in England as late as the 1870s, and tutorial classes for non-traditional students were established first in England in 1908 as the result of the noted Oxford Conference of 1907.

The university extension idea and its practical implementation soon spread throughout the English-speaking world and took firm root there. In line with different social and economic conditions and development in the English-speaking countries since the turn of the century, both the concept and its application developed in somewhat different directions. The most broad understanding of university extension, of community service and of the involvement of the universities in adult education evolved in North America, leading to a flamboyant expansion of this part of the university activity in the 1960s With the largely unexpected economic downturn in the last few years, most of the flamboyance of the North American university continuing education is gone and cracks are beginning to show in the commitment of the universities to continuing education, which until recently has been taken for granted.

The University and Adult Education

The typical North American broad provision of university continuing education encompasses (1) general non-credit continuing education in the humanities and the sciences, (2) professional continuing education, (3) part-time degree credit study, (4) training of adult educators and (5) research in adult education. Community service is sometimes subsumed under continuing education, while other times continuing education is seen as part of community service. Specific institutions vary in the degree to which they provide all five of these aspects of comprehensive university continuing education, but it is safe to claim that every North American university has a commitment to part-time degree credit study.

The English university extension idea also found its way to continental Europe in the 1880s. There were some early promising beginnings of university extension in the Hapsburg Empire around the turn of the century ; the Vienna University established extension lectures in 1893, followed by the Innsbruck University in 1897 and Graz University in 1898. However, this movement did not find its way into the other German-speaking countries. In Northern Europe, summer extension courses were established in Sweden in the early 1890s, and in 1898 Lund University set up a regional Central Bureau for Popular Science Lectures. Attempts in Denmark in the late 1890s to get the Copenhagen University involved remained unsuccessful. Western and Southern Europe remained barren in this respect. The European university extension development was halted by the First World War, and the European universities as institutions have, until fairly recently, remained very aloof from the provision of continuing education.

One of the reasons why general university extension did not take root in continental Europe is the existence of alternative provision. A number of institutions and voluntary associations, most of which are completely separate and independent from the universities proper (although they rely to a significant extent on university faculty to deliver their programs) and whose primary, if not sole, purpose is the provision of adult education, were established in most European countries in the nineteenth and early twentieth century. Some of these, like the people's universities in Scandinavia and Eastern Europe operate to a considerable extent as de-facto university extension departments. Another important factor is the traditional, and in many

European countries still widespread, intellectual elitism of the universities.

During the last twenty-five years, the European universities have been induced, to a varying degree, to get involved in the provision of continuing education. This started at first with general non-credit lectures and courses. Lately the universities are beginning to provide continuing professional education. Part-time degree credit programs still are rather rare in Western Europe, but are widespread in the East. University training programs for adult educators are well developed in most East European countries, while in the West such programs are well established only in the Federal Republic of Germany and the Netherlands. Research in adult education in continental Europe is carried out just as often in major independent research institutes as in the universities.

University continuing education
University administrators and the academic community on the whole have come to accept three responsibilities for the university : teaching, research and community service. Of these, the extension of teaching to other than the traditional fulltime students, and community service, are both the most recent and the least developed. Among academics there are two strongly held views of this expanding role for the university. There are those to whom the university must remain separate and independent from any direct responsibility to society, if it is to truly serve society through critical appraisal and diagnosis of its failings. Then there are those who have a strong commitment not only to basic research, critical analysis and diagnosis of the ills of society, but who desire to go beyond to direct application of research, prescription and cure. Thus while to the first, 'splendid isolation' is the norm, involvement and even activism is the life blood to the others. In my view the position appropriate to the university in the Western world in the late twentieth century is to retain sufficient measure of independence from the vagaries of changing governments and fickle popular trends, but only so that it can serve as an independent but responsible institution bringing to bear its unique resources of research and knowledge base, of critical analysis, and of dissemination of knowledge, beyond the walls of the university to assist society and individuals in the solution of

problems and challenges facing us all.

The most recent role of the university contributing to the development of society and individuals within it through the provision of continuing education and community service will increasingly be demanded by society of which the university is a part, and the university needs to respond, both for altruistic and for self-interest reasons.

Even just a cursory analysis of the development of Western society since the 1940s will provide multiple reasons for the university not only to be involved in continuing education and community service, but to afford these areas increasing priority and resources. Among these reasons can be counted philosophical reasons, social reasons, political reasons, economic reasons, demographic reasons and self-interest reasons.

Given that the university accepts as its two major roles the generation and dissemination of knowledge, there is no apparent reason why the dissemination should be restricted to full-time undergraduate and graduate students and not be extended to university alumni as well as to those adults in society who, although they may not have a university degree, can benefit from the intellectual stimulation and personal enrichment only a university can provide.

Society created the university because the church and the state needed clerics and clerks with advanced education. Later on the university gained an increasing measure of independence, almost in line with the growth of and refinement of scientific inquiry and knowledge. With the growing complexity of social, political and economic structure of society and the explosion of knowledge, the university became a unique and indispensable institution without which modern society could not function. The university today is the only institution imbued with the values of objective intellectual inquiry and social criticism based on research. The larger society, not only the narrow academic community, needs to benefit from these values.

At a time when public expenditures increasingly are questioned and coming under close scrutiny, and when the university budget is being cut back everywhere, the university needs much broader political support than it had in the past. Both continuing education and community service bring the university and the community closer together and through their provision the university gains considerable support in the larger community and through it more positive influence on government decisions.

The current rapid technological and structural economic changes affect all segments of society. This brings the growing need for understanding the change, adapting to it or resisting it where it is harmful, and being able to cope with it. Again, the university has unique resources which can and must be brought to bear on this area in policy formulation, developing informed and responsible citizenry and in professional development.

The ongoing demographic and social changes in the developed world will require the university to adjust to new constituencies and their needs. Among the new constituencies are the mature non-employed adults who seek personal enrichment through study, the wage earners who seek to enhance their knowledge and skills in liberal arts, the professionals who seek to maintain and update their professional knowledge and skills. The decreasing 18-24 year cohort, the general ageing of the population and the increasing number of women entering credit and non-credit university continuing education will have considerable impact on the universities. The characteristics, both social and psychological, of the clientele will require of the universities changes and adjustments in organization, approaches, financing, and provision of programs and services, with respect to both, part-time degree study and non-credit continuing education.

Since Bora Samolovcev in his paper deals with training of adult educators and research in adult education, I will limit the rest of my paper to part-time degree study, to non-credit continuing education, both in general knowledge and in professional development, and to community service.

Part-time degree credit
Teaching is next to research an accepted major responsibility of the university. Until the mid-twentieth century, except for a few rare situations, teaching was limited to full-time graduate and undergraduate students. With the demographic, social, economic and political changes since the Second World War, part-time degree study opportunities began to appear, at first in North America and East Europe and later on in the United Kingdom and some countries in Western Europe.

The University and Adult Education

The introduction of the unit credit system in the United States early in this century laid the foundation for part-time degree study. However, it was not until the 1940s before this potential was realized and began to be implemented; up until then the universities were primarily serving only full-time students. By the late 1950s, many universities had established separate evening colleges for part-time students. By the late 1970s, part-time students in credit programs formed approximately one third of the student body in North America, and it is possible now to complete first degrees, and a number of graduate degrees, by part-time study.

In continental Europe, opportunities for part-time degree study were introduced first in the Soviet Union, between the two world wars. There was a gradual shift from full-time to part-time study and since the 1950s a widespread network of separate evening and correspondence faculties has been established in the Soviet Union, offering parallel degree programs which generally take only one year longer than full-time study to complete. In addition, there are some 600 correspondence divisions in regular higher education institutions. This total enterprise serves in excess of 600,000 students. This practice has been adopted in all East European countries, and part-time study is fostered and supported by the state and the Communist party as desirable both economically and socially. Correspondence and distance education are by far the most prevalent types of part-time degree study in East Europe. While part-time degree study is still popular and enjoys widespread state support in the Soviet Union and the German Democratic Republic, it is being increasingly questioned in the other East European countries, especially in Czechoslovakia and to some extent also in Hungary and Poland.

In Western Europe, Sweden is the leader in opening the universities to mature students. Part-time degree study there is possible through evening classes, single subject courses, off-campus courses, university study circles (until 1983), summer university, and decentralized distance education. In other parts of Western Europe, part-time degree study provision still is in very rudimentary stages of development. Among the notable exceptions is the <u>Université de Paris VIII</u> established in 1968 to serve primarily employed students through the provision of evening and weekend courses. Planned originally for 6,000 students, it now enrols in excess of 30,000, most of whom work either full-time or part-time. Part-time degree study still is rather the exception in the United Kingdom, except for the Open University which was founded in 1969 to serve mature students.

The establishment of the Open University in England gave an impetus to similar development in a number of continental European countries, where the traditional universities also have been reluctant or unwilling to serve adult part-time students. Thus the Universidad Nacional de Educación a Distancia was established in Spain in 1972; the Fernuniversität-Gesamthochschule Hagen in the Federal Republic of Germany in 1974; and the Open University of the Netherlands in 1981. It is significant to note that since its establishment in 1969, the Open University in the United Kingdom graduated more than 50,000 students.

Any account of the access of adults to degree completion would not be adequate without at least a mention of the examination challenge available in most European countries for many years, most usually in the form of Externistenprüfung. This practice has been brought to perfection in the external degree of the University of London (established in 1856 and since 1858 available solely on the basis of examinations), and the Regents External Degree of the University of the State of New York (established in 1971 and based on the recognition of independent learning).

Having provided a brief overview and some examples of the development and current provision of part-time degree study, I would like to ask now "why should the university be involved in this type of extension?".

Teaching, next to knowledge generation and research, is an unquestioned responsibility of the university. With the increasing complexity of modern technological society we need adequate numbers of citizens with higher education experience, both in the technical professions and in the humanities and social sciences. The universities have to respond to this need, or they will be bypassed. Due to a variety of factors, among these social, economic, demographic and political, it no longer is possible and appropriate to meet this increasing need only through full-time study. In every jurisdiction where the universities have introduced possibilities for part-time degree study, the number of part-time degree students has increased dramatically. While the universities must ensure that part-time degree study is of the same quality as full-time degree study, they no longer have adequate grounds to reject it. Furthermore, there is now sufficient evidence that universities in fact benefit, both intellectually and economically, from part-time students.

General non-credit continuing education
General non-credit continuing education, extension of the university liberal education in the humanities and sciences, was the first interface between the university and non-traditional adult students. As I already have mentioned, this type of university extension originated in the United Kingdom in the 1870s and spread from there to many countries. However, it took root in any significant measure only in the English-speaking world. Until the late 1950s it remained the main thrust of university continuing education.

Today, university general non-credit continuing education still is very strong in the United Kingdom, in Australia and in New Zealand. In North America, the universities in the western states and provinces have a long tradition of provision of broadly based continuing education programs, with thriving general education, while in the eastern states and provinces this is not the case. The best examples of broad comprehensive provision of university continuing education are the University of California at Los Angeles, the University of Alberta and the University of British Columbia.

University extension took root in post-war Germany in 1956, with seminar courses at Göttingen University, followed by similar development at the Berlin Free University. However before non-credit general education could spread and become established, the direction in West Germany turned towards provision of professional continuing education by the universities. Today, most of the university level general continuing education in West Germany is not organized directly by the universities, but rather by the 'Volkshochschulen' and other non-university institutions, with the universities providing lecturers through their 'Kontaktstellen für wissenschaftliche Weiterbildung'.

The situation is similar in East Europe, where such programs are organized by lecture societies outside the universities and by peoples' or workers' universities. It is expected of the members of the intelligentsia, and accepted as a responsibility by them, to volunteer to give popularizing lectures through these institutions.

In Northern Europe, extensive provision of university level lectures and courses by the many voluntary study associations, much of this staffed by university students and faculty, created a situation in which until fairly recently direct university involvement was not required, and to an extent even resisted by the voluntary associations.

An interesting type of non-credit general continuing education are the 'summer universities'. These are usually one to two week long residential intensive courses, often on a special topic. Such universities are organized in Finland and in Hungary. In Finland these universities started in about 1912. Now there are about 20 such universities in Finland, with some 40,000 adults participating each year. In many ways these programs are very similar to the summer courses organized by many of the universities in the United Kingdom.

The post-war demographic shift in the Western world brought about the development of the 'université du troisième âge'. The first of these universities was established in Toulouse in France in 1973. By 1980 such continuing education programs for retired people were established by Dortmund and by Marburg University in West Germany. Today there are third age universities also in Belgium, Hungary, Italy, Poland, Spain, Sweden, Switzerland and the U.K. With the growing numbers of older people, and with their increasing sophistication and political awareness, these third age universities will have a significant impact both on the universities and on society.

Having outlined the roots and development of university non-credit general continuing education, and given some examples of its current manifestation, I would like to conclude also this section with the question of "why should the university be involved in this type of extension?"

I have already stated that generation and dissemination of knowledge are generally accepted tasks of the university. It is only logical, given the generally increased educational level of the adult population, to extend the dissemination of knowledge to adults who are not registered credit students at the university. The modern complex democratic society, unlike its medieval counterpart, depends on the knowledge and understanding, as well as social and political skills and awareness, of its citizenry. Through contributing to the advancement of the general level of education of the adult population, the university can enhance the quality of life of the society of which it is a part. Only the university has the resources for intellectual stimulation of society ; these resources must not be restricted to the small academic community, if the university itself is not to suffer. Finally, through its intellectual and artistic resources open to the larger society, the university can contribute significantly to individual enrichment and to the social and cultural life of the society.

Let me close this part of my paper by stressing that the non-credit general continuing education programs offered by the university must not be restricted only to university graduates or those who can gain admission to the degree credit programs of the university. The non-credit programs must be open to all adults, who <u>in their own view</u> can benefit from participating in the program.

Professional continuing education
Professional continuing education anywhere is a fairly recent phenomenon. The need for this branch of university continuing education was brought about by the accelerating expansion of knowledge in all professional areas since the Second World War. Today, a professional must update and refresh his or her knowledge and skills regularly, if he or she is to remain effective.

In some professions, where the outdated skills or knowledge of the professional might become dangerous to the client, especially in the health sciences, but even in the legal profession and engineering, professional associations or the state have issued regulations prescribing compulsory continuing professional education as a condition of remaining licensed. This trend has developed farthest in the United States. This is seen as a boon by some adult educators and institutions providing upgrading and refresher programs, while it is being abhorred and decried as an attack on the very roots of adult education by others.

Professional continuing education is provided in some jurisdictions by the universities, while in others it is the professional associations which are the provider. Ideally, professional continuing education should be voluntary and provided in close cooperation between the appropriate professional school of the university and the professional association.

In the early stages in the development of professional continuing education, occasional courses were offered in a haphazard fashion, usually when an innovation or new legislation caught the attention of the profession or the provider. Since the 1960s, professional continuing education took firm root in North America and expanded rapidly in all states and provinces, often spurred on by legislation. Today it forms by far the largest part of the university continuing education in North America. In Europe this development did not occur on any scale until the 1970s; in most European countries it is still in the experimental or model stages.

In North America there is today no university which would not be involved in the provision of professional continuing education. The magnitude of the enterprise can be illustrated by my own university which provides programs in agriculture, architecture, commerce and business management, dentistry, education, engineering, forestry, law, medicine, nursing, pharmacy, social work, and urban and regional planning. These programs attract some 40,000 registrations per year. This level of provision is fairly typical of the large North American university. Professor Cyril Houle of the University of Chicago wrote the definitive study of the rationale for and ways and means of professional continuing education (HOULE, 1980).

West Germany is the most advanced in professional continuing education in Western Europe, with legislation mandating and directing the universities to provide access to professionals to continuing education. In Northern Europe, Norway and Sweden are the most advanced ; this is the result of the university reforms in these countries in the 1970s. In Sweden this provision is best developed in the field of in-service training for teachers, which is provided in each one of the six university regions. In Norway the regional colleges and many of the university institutes provide rather extensive programs of courses and seminars for professionals.

The East European countries, with their planned economy systems and post-war efforts at rapid industrialization, are providing substantial university programs in this area. This provision is best developed in the Soviet Union and Romania. Much of this is accomplished through part-time degree study used as professional development. In Romania and Hungary, ministries have been made responsible for the planning and provision of vocational and professional upgrading within their sector, drawing on the universities for instructional resources. In Yugoslavia, most of the professional development is organized through the workers' universities and work places rather than through the universities proper.

In France, Centres for Continuing Education were established in the universities in 1972, as a result of the Law of July 1971. In my view it is unfortunate that these centres do not receive any funding from the budget of the university and more recently are seen by the university administrations as money-makers for the university (This opinion, regrettably, is also spreading in other countries in Europe and even in North America, where until recently continuing education was considered as one of the functions of the university in need and worthy of support from general funds.)

The situation is quite different in West Germany, where the universities are required to provide lecturers to other institutions at no cost. A very important and unique aspect of university professional continuing education in West Germany is the requirement that the university provide professional development for its own scientific, academic and other staff. To my knowledge this is the only country where such regulation exists. In 1983 the universities organized 766 courses with all together 10,671 participants (KOMMER, 1984).

Another interesting variation on the provision of professional continuing education can be found in Sweden. At the University of Uppsala, rather than organizing separate continuing education courses and seminars, the University makes it possible for professionals to participate in regular degree credit courses, without necessarily being registered in a degree program and proceeding towards completion of a degree.

The Netherlands opted for a model of professional continuing education organized at the national level by independent professional continuing education associations (a separate association for each profession), which cooperate very closely with the universities and draw on them for expertise and resources.

Given the typical organization of professional

continuing education, which is based on very compartmentalized and specialized professions and subject matter, it is very easy for the program to slip into training rather than education. The most important elements, which most often are missing from the program, are interprofessional programs and liberal education. Yet, in our complex society no professional can work effectively in isolation, and in areas such as health promotion and environmental protection nowadays the team approach to problem solving is the norm. This is very rarely reflected in continuing education programs. Similarly, if we are not to degenerate into a technocratic society, governed by specialists without a broad general understanding, we have to provide adequate liberal education as an integral part of professional continuing education.

To conclude this part of my paper, let me again ask the question of "why should the university be involved in this type of extension?"

Similar to my rationale for the involvement of the university in non-credit general continuing education as a logical extension of its tasks of dissemination of knowledge, the professional schools have, in my view, a direct responsibility for life-long professional development of graduates in their profession. I have already pointed out that updating of the professional is crucial ; the university, as the most important institution in society with resources for research and further development of professional skills and techniques, has to accept its responsibility in this area. Furthermore, the university and its academic staff have a great deal to gain from this symbiotic relationship with the professionals in the field, both in terms of opportunities for testing out models and conducting field research and in building up important political support base for the university.

Centralized/decentralized organization
At this point I would like to consider briefly the issue of centralized vs. decentralized organization of university continuing education. This issue is at the centre of vigorous debate in North America, but is beginning also to appear in some European countries.

Historically, university extension was a centralized function of one department, acting on behalf of the entire university. This went without challenge as long as university extension involved itself mainly with general education non-credit (and later also part-time degree credit) programs. When professional continuing education made its appearance, and especially after it took firm root in the university with the help of the central extension departments, the professional schools became interested and often took over professional continuing education in their profession. The Medical Schools were the first to develop their own continuing education programs and, to my knowledge, there is not today a university in North America where continuing medical education would be part of the central department. In those European countries where the professional schools are independent universities this is not an organizational problem, but it is an issue now in those countries which developed comprehensive universities such as the 'Gesamthochschule'.

The advocates of the decentralized model claim that when continuing education is decentralized into faculties and departments, it becomes more an integral function and tends to get more support. The professional schools also see it as a valuable link with the profession, which they would rather maintain directly from the school than via a central department.

The advocates of the centralized model, while not denying the benefits pointed out by the decentralists, believe that if left to faculties and departments, continuing education will not enjoy the high profile it needs and which it will receive from central administration. They claim that 'what is everybody's business is nobody's business' and that there is a need for a central department whose sole responsibility is the provision of continuing education, and which has a specific line item budget for this function.

Among other factors which need to be considered is the need for interdisciplinary and interprofessional approaches in continuing education, for as the writers of the CERI report <u>The University and the Community</u> put it, "communities have problems, universities have departments" (CERI, 1982). Another important factor is that the university as an institution is more than a sum total of its parts, and that it, not only its faculties and departments, needs to be committed to continuing education.

The University and Adult Education

Community service
Having dealt with non-credit general and professional continuing education, let me share with you a few thoughts about community service. As I have mentioned at the beginning, community service is sometimes subsumed under continuing education, while other times continuing education is seen as part of community service. In my considered view, continuing education, both non-credit general education and professional development, is an integral part of the academic teaching role of the university, extended to new tasks and new clientele - it is not community service. (It is exactly the thinking that continuing education is community service that makes it an appendage, a charity, a lesser and expendable function and that enables the university not to meet its full responsibility in this area.) On the other hand, parts or aspects of community service can be, and often are, integrated organizationally into administrative units responsible for continuing education, while other aspects of community service relate directly to the research function of the university or are incidental benefits to the community of the resources, both human and physical, of the university located in its midst.

Among the areas where continuing education and community service overlap is the variety of educational counselling centres for adults established by many universities. Thus for example my university established in 1973 the UBC Women's Resources Centre. Acting as a catalyst - stimulating women to get from where they are to where they want to be - and providing information and motivation is the ongoing mission of the Centre. Some 12,000 women each year obtain peer counselling services in life planning and vocational counselling. Many of them also avail themselves of the psychological testing provided by the Centre. The UBC Women's Resources Centre became a model for similar centres established in the regional colleges. It also serves as placement of graduate students in Educational Counselling, Nursing, Adult Education and Social Work for practicums.

The participation of the university or of its parts in community development is an example of symbiosis between pure and applied research, continuing education and community service. The university is among the very few institutions in modern society which can bring its objective and neutral research knowledge and resources to bear on problems faced by the community. Continuing education serves as an important link between the researchers and the community and facilitates understanding of basic principles and involvement and participation in the community development project. Through combining research and continuing education the university can function as an honest broker in solving a particular problem and thus provide a valuable service to the community.

The 'science workshops', which had their origin in the Netherlands in the 1970s, and which now exist also in a number of universities in France and the United Kingdom, are a good example of the combination of the research function of the university and community service. "They evolved out of complaints that science had become excessively elitist and out of touch with social problems... Their goal is to provide a means for members of the public to seek answers to scientific and technical questions arising from their daily lives, and for scientists and engineers to apply their knowledge, training, and skills to topics of social concern" (DICKINSON, 1984).

Among the incidental benefits to the community from university resources are important cultural services such as art exhibits, concerts, theatre performances and readings provided by the university and open to the public. Many universities also have facilities such as museums, observatories, demonstration farms, research forests, and industrial plant models, from which industry as well as general public can benefit. Finally, physical university resources such as classrooms, laboratories, theatres, concert halls, swimming pools, gymnasia and often student residences are made available to the public as a community service.

Envoi
In my paper I have outlined the rationale for and need of university involvement in lifelong learning and in provision of continuing education, and of the benefits resulting both to the university and the community. In my view, in the current economic and social situation in the developed world, we need more, not less, provision of university continuing education. I trust that the recent setbacks it seems to be suffering throughout Europe and North America in university commitment and support are just temporary aberrations in the evolution of the university.

The University and Adult Education

Throughout its history, the university has changed in order to serve new needs brought about by the evolution of society and expansion of science, while it at the same time has guarded vigorously the basic tenets of freedom, objectivity and independence from the vagaries of governments. It is this tension and balance between adaptation and resistance which made the university as social institution survive for centuries. I trust that the university will survive and adapt creatively also to the most recent challenge of lifelong learning and the learning society. Continuing education will play a crucial role in this.

REFERENCES

Alford, H. (ed.) (1980) Power and Conflict in Continuing Education, Wadsworth Pub. Co., Belmont
Allesh, J. (ed.) (1983) Berufsbezogene wissenschaftliche Weiterbildung an den Hochschulen : Perspektiven und Modelle, Bock, Bad Honnef
Der Bundesminister für Bildung und Wissenschaft (1982) Weiterbildungsaufgaben der Hochschulen, Bock, Bonn
Campbell, D.D. (1984) The New Majority : Adult Learners in the University, The University of Alberta Press, Edmonton
Carnegie Council on Policy Studies in Higher Education (1981) Three Thousand Futures : The Next Twenty Years for Higher Education, Jossey-Bass, San Francisco
CERI (1982) The University and the Community : The Problems of Changing Relationships, OECD, Paris
Cropley, A.J. (1979) Lifelong Education : A Stocktaking, Unesco Institute for Education, Hamburg
Dickinson, D. (1984) 'Science Shops' Flourish in Europe, Science, 223, 4641
Faure, E. et al. (1972) Learning to Be, Unesco, Paris
Houle, C.O. (1972) The Design of Education, Jossey-Bass, San Francisco
----- (1980) Continuing Learning in the Professions, Jossey-Bass, San Francisco
Kommer, A. (1984) 'Die gegenwärtige Situation der Weiterbildung des Hochschulpersonals', Hochschule und Weiterbildung, 2
Krüger, W. (ed.) (1978) Universität und Erwachsenenbildung in Europa, Georg Westermann Verlag, Braunschweig

----- (1982) *Wissenschaft, Hochschule und Erwachsenenbildung*, Georg Westermann Verlag, Braunschweig

Kulich, J. (1982) 'Lifelong Education and the Universities : A Canadian Perspective', *International Journal of Lifelong Education*, 1, 2

Kulich, J. and Krüger, W. (eds) (1980) *The Universities and Adult Education in Europe*, The University of British Columbia, Centre for Continuing Education, Vancouver

----- (1986) 'University Level Adult Education in East Europe', To be published in *International Journal of University Adult Education*.

Lengrand, P. (1975) *An Introduction to Lifelong Education*, Unesco Press, Paris

Lenz, W. and Schrantz, M. (1984) *Öffnung der Universität*, Institut für Erziehungswissenschaft der Universität Innsbruck, Innsbruck

Österreichisches Bundesministerium für Wissenschaft und Forschung, *Weiterbildung an der Universität*, BMWF, Wien

Peters, J.M. et al. (1980) *Building an Effective Adult Education Enterprise*, Jossey-Bass, San Francisco

Peterson, R.E. et al. (1979) *Lifelong Learning in America*, Jossey-Bass, San Francisco

Sensky, K. et al. (1980) *Universitäre Erwachsenenbildung*, Thomas Morus Akademie, Bensberg

Stephens, M.D. and Roderick, G.W. (eds) (1975) *Universities for a Changing World : The Role of the University in the Late Twentieth Century*, David and Charles, London

Stern, M.R. (1983) *Power and Conflict in Continuing Professional Education*, Wadsworth Pub. Co, Belmont

Teather, D.C.B. (ed.) (1982) *Towards the Community University*, Kogan Page, London

Thornton, A.H. and Stephens, M.D. (eds) (1977) *The University in its Region : The Extra-Mural Contribution*, Department of Adult Education, University of Nottingham, Nottingham

UNESCO (1984) *World-wide Inventory of non-traditional Post-secondary Educational Institutions*, Unesco, Paris

----- (1985) 'University Level Adult Education in Scandinavia', *Canadian Journal of University Continuing Education*, 11, 2

Verner, C. and Booth, A. (1964) *Adult Education*, The Center for Applied Research in Education, Washington, D.C.

The University and Adult Education

Wissenschaftsrat (1983) <u>Empfehlungen zur Weiterbildung an den Hochschulen</u>, Wissenschaftsrat, Köln

Chapter Thirteen
TRAINING SYSTEMS FOR FUTURE ADULT EDUCATORS

Borivoj SAMOLOVČEV
Univ. of Belgrade
Yugoslavia

The challenges of the 1990s without doubt are being taken seriously also in the field of adult education, especially at the higher education level and in the academic orientation. Basically these challenges are already present, especially in the context of the technological developments as well as in widespread broader social processes, and more and more within the educational processes. There is a tendency in all modern countries of even further development, without regard for the global orientation of their particular socio-political system. Higher education for adults, which in its complexity consists of formal and non-formal adult education, is part of this process. The scientific andragogical ideas, which are based to a high degree on the well developed multidisciplinary scientific system, operate within the context of this social development.

With the developing educational practice, as well as with the accumulation and differentiation of the andragogical scientific knowledge, came the need for qualification and training of professional adult educators/andragogues. This need can be evidenced since the second half of the nineteenth century - from N.F.S. Grundtvig and A. Mansbridge to the present - as I will show in a brief overview.

Brief overview of the development of the training of adult educators
The beginnings of the qualification process for adult educators can be seen in experiential learning, that is in the intensive participation in the educational process and through it the imperceptible internalization of certain didactic principles, norms and behaviour. In my view, the first occur-

rence of this can be observed in the practice of the Danish folk high schools where the role of the teacher could be assumed only by those who themselves have attended these schools, who have fully experienced their milieu. This principle applies to a certain degree in Denmark up to today.

Similar adult educator qualification attempts can be observed also in the United Kingdom with the advent of extra-mural work and university extension. The W.E.A. actualized this especially with the beginning of the tutorial classes in 1907. Also this way of working, which was in its time of significance, demanded a corresponding qualification of the adult educators which could at that time be acquired only from learning by experience. Similar occurrence can be seen also in the early phase of agricultural extension in the United States. From such early beginnings developed later on the systematical non-degree qualification of adult educators, which today is the most common training system in many countries.

The training of adult educators in degree programs did not start until considerably later on. I have traced its first appearance to Poland between the two world wars, when Helen Radlińska (RADLIŃSKA, 1947) established it within the framework of social pedagogy. This was based on a social-pedagogical orientation in adult education and in the training of adult educators, which also continued after the end of the Second World War. Thus already in 1946 three Polish universities (Krakow, Lodz and Warsaw) organized training programs for adult educators after the Radlinska theoretical concept (SAMOLOVČEV, 1963, p. 59). Then in the early 1960s occurred the scientific polarization of the theory of adult education in Poland into the social-pedagogical and the andragogical orientation. This found expression also in the training of adult educators.

In the period after the Second World War, as early as in the 1950s, the development of training programs for adult educators intensified and broadened. The United States assumed a leadership position in this development, and as early as in 1960 there already were in the U.S. well developd masters' and doctoral training programs for adult educators at 12 universities. According to Cyril O. Houle, in 1968 such programs had been in operation at 20 universities in the United States and Canada (SMITH et al., 1970, p. 116). These programs are clearly differentiated in their conceptualization and thus also in their scientific orientation. The two main approaches are the educational and the sociological perspective. The educational perspective programs prepare adult education professionals as educators, without differentiation between their prospective specific employment (such as agricultural extension or university continuing education). The University of Wisconsin and The University of Chicago are representative examples. The sociological perspective programs, on the other hand, (as represented by the University of California at Berkeley), concentrate on leisure time and leisure time activities and on social educational work. The fundamental content areas in the training programs are, next to subjects such as rural sociology and sociology of leisure, philosophy of adult education, history of adult education, adult psychology, adult learning, program planning, etc. Individual and group research projects receive special attention. The development of andragogy as a discipline and the changes in the structure of educational need bring about naturally also changes in direction, organization and style of training of adult educators. This is imminent in the training of and continuing education for adult educators in the United States as well as in other countries with such training programs.

Due to the intensive post-war development of adult education practice and theory in the United Kingdom, training programs at the master's and doctoral level were also established and expanded there. Since the basis for these training programs is the need for and expansion of the practice of adult education, several directions and programs have evolved in the U.K.:

1. training of adult education generalists;
2. training of community development specialists;
3. training of industrial trainers, and
4. training of social adult education specialists.

The content areas covered in the training of adult education generalists, for example in the program at the University of Glasgow, are as follows :

1. global adult education system;
2. history of adult education;
3. psychology of adult learning;
4. adult instruction;

5. principles of adult education, and
6. comparative adult education.

In addition to the above, some universities also offer other courses, such as :

7. organization and planning of adult education ;
8. sociological foundations of adult education, and;
9. evaluation and research methods.

The content areas in the training of community development specialists usually include the following :

1. development and organization of community life in the U.K.;
2. psychology and techniques of communication ;
3. social action, and
4. adult basic education.

The training of industrial trainers, to use the example of the University of Manchester, includes :

1. industrial sociology;
2. industrial psychology;
3. organizational theory;
4. planning, structure and evaluation of industrial training;
5. educational technology, and
6. research methods.

The training of social adult education specialists, as for example at the University of Southampton, contains :

1. methods of social education;
2. social policies and leadership;
3. human development and behaviour;
4. sociology;
5. legal system;
6. social philosophy;
7. criminology, and
8. civil law.

The training in the four streams outlined above is organized primarily as part-time study through individual and group work at the level of diploma and master's programs. The special attention given to field visits, study tours and research projects undoubtedly contributes to the qualitative and functional qualification of the trainees.

The Netherlands, with their original approaches, bring a significant contribution to the development of degree programs in adult education. Several training programs developed from the work of Dr. Ten Have and his followers ; I will mention the programs at the University of Amsterdam and the University of Nijmegen.

The program at the University of Amsterdam was developed on the basis of the andragological concept of the theory of adult education. The approach employed combines eclectically the andragological and the social education perspectives in three study fields established in the 1970s :

1. adult education in its original meaning;
2. adult education in the life of the community, and
3. social education.

All of these three fields find their manifestation in :

1. work in adult education institutions (folk high schools, residential folk high schools, evening schools, continuing education centres and community centres) and
2. work in social education institutions.

The University of Nijmegen offers a similar comprehensive 5-years program in andragology, leading to a doctorate. The basic 3-year sub-program includes :

1. educational work in the labour unions;
2. educational aspects of neighbourhood community development;
3. emancipatory program planning for women, and
4. political education with young adults.

During the study process, special attention is given to work in project and work groups and to group research projects (GIESCHLER, 1977, pp. 44-6), which is without doubt an interesting innovation.

Original adult education training programs have been developed also in the Federal Republic of Germany, a country with extraordinary scientific pedagogical tradition. There are differences among programs in the highly developed training system, however, in my view, these differences are more marked in their study/program concept than in the scientific concept. I will use as examples the Ruhr University Bochum and the Free University of Berlin.

The Ruhr University Bochum, in harmony with its systemic scientific view of adult education, organized its training program on the basis of the classical scientific pedagogical system, within which there is a combination of the practical pedagogy and its two constituent disciplines - that of adult education and that of an academic discipline. This perception of adult education is currently manifested more and more as adult pedagogy, with developed philosophical, historical and didactical sphere ; this is illustrated in Die Einführung in die Erwachsenenbildung (KNOLL, 1973). In the study of adult pedagogy, psychology of adult learning and research methods are given an important place.

The adult pedagogy orientation is present also at the Free University of Berlin, where it is, however, also combined with a very dynamic study approach which combines teaching and research, as outlined by Dr. Fritz Borinski in 1968 (OLBRICH, 1977, p. 6) : "As in all disciplines, the aim is to unite teaching and research, to unite scientific education and practical professional training. Those who teach adult education, through lectures or seminars, should be closely connected with it both in their research and practice. Those being prepared by the universities for the adult education field should during their studies be introduced to research as well as to practice". In this orientation of the training program, both the theory and history of worker's education and the instructional and didactic problems of adult education are researched in a multitude of short term seminars which have a flexible structure. This model of training and study surely will never lose its timeliness. On the contrary, it will always remain up-to-date and lively.

The expansion of adult education, and with it of the scientific andragogical idea, led in Yugoslavia to the establishment of a specific higher education system of training of adult educators. What are the characteristics of the scientific development and of the current situation of this training system in Yugoslavia?

Two basic developmental phases mark the degree training programs for adult educators since the establishment of the first such program at the University of Belgrade in 1964 :

1. the phase of the specialization streaming and
2. the phase of the guided independent study.

This led to the development of two parallel basic training systems, both of which are in operation today.

The first training system, the specialization streaming type, developed further and remained within the framework of pedagogical studies. In this type of training, adult education specialization starts in the third year and lasts two semesters. The specialization streaming program ends with a Diploma in Education (Adult Education) (bachelor's degree). Originally this training program prepared generalists in adult education, while currently it is aimed primarily at industrial trainers. The following adult education subjects form the scientific basis of this training system :

1. general andragogy, with philosophical, sociological, psychological and didactic basis of adult education (three courses);
2. industrial andragogy (Universities of Skoplje, Zagreb, and Ljubljana);
3. theoretical and methodological foundations of socialization (University of Skoplje);
4. comparative andragogy (Universities of Skoplje, Zagreb and Ljubljana), and
5. research methodologies for aligned disciplines which form a part of the basic study of andragogy.

In addition, some of the universities also offer special seminars in adult education, such as andragogy in social work or theory and practice of adult education in Yugoslavia (ŠOLJAN, 1985, pp. 243-6).

As can be seen from the above outline of the study program in this type of training, two directions of university study of adult education developed in Yugoslavia :

1. the direction of training of adult education generalists, and
2. the direction of training of industrial trainers.

However, as these two profiles of professional adult

educators have not yet been sufficiently validated in practice, it is not at this stage possible to establish the efficacy of such profiles.

The second training system phase, that of guided independent study of adult education, was introduced in the 1980s at the Faculty of Arts of the University of Belgrade. This 4-year study also draws significantly on basic pedagogical disciplines. Its broad curricular basis reaches into all fundamental aspects of adult education : basic education, vocational education, social-educational work (re-education), and educational planning. This curriculum aims at the preparation of adult education generalists, however, with the provision of specialization in the 7th semester (penology, Marxist education, organization of educational and cultural work). Special attention is given to individual and group research projects.

Graduate study in adult education, both at the master's and doctoral level, is organized very similarly at almost all the universities (Zagreb, Ljubljana, Skoplje, and Belgrade). The 2-year M.A. program includes the following :

1. general andragogy;
2. comparative andragogy;
3. psychology of adult learning;
4. research methods, and
5. foreign language.

Tutorial system, combined with group research projects and seminars, predominates as the study form at the graduate level.

In spite of the 22-year experience with university training of adult educators in Yugoslavia, the two key questions concerning this training have not been answered :

1. whether this training system at the undergraduate and graduate level should be developed further, and
2. whether such training should aim at producing generalists or specialists.

Currently we still do not have a firm answer to these questions.

Conceptual questions of modern training of adult educators

The recent development of systems of training of adult educators throughout the world has led to a closer agreement in the scientific rationale for this activity. As far as organization of such training and of methods and techniques used in various countries are concerned, there still are marked differences. These are noticeable especially in undergraduate and post-graduate training programs and are in general determined by national pedagogical and higher education traditions. These kinds of differences, which are not of a substantive nature, will persist for a long time yet. However, the substantive and the common element of all these training systems is at this junction how we can find, in the framework of andragogy and thus in the educative processes, the answer to the challenge of our times, especially in the context of adult education. I am convinced that the search for these answers should be a joint quest, first and foremost in the area of general andragogy which is the key to the scientific way of the training of adult educators.

In the current higher education of adults, in contrast to earlier periods of modern adult education, the central problem of this educational activity, the forever actual ontological and the question of the valuable, appears deeper and broader also in the framework of andragogy (although in somewhat newer philosophical relationships as was pointed out in the opening paper by Walter Leirman). These relationships determine more directly and pointedly the clash of two ideas - the idea "to be" and the idea "to be something", the clash between two philosophical directions - that of universal humanity and that of pragmatical-successful individuality. For the first idea, those values which in a way are timeless - as this was pointed out in Yugoslavia by Dr. Nedjeljko Kujundžić (KUJUNDŽIĆ, 1979) - will be more and more : freedom, humanity, initiative, selfhood, versatility, inquisitiveness, spirit, drive, industriousness. All these are values which possess, in spite of differing concepts of their basic core, ontological and pedagogical actuality. This is especially the case in our own time, (referred to as the technological period, which is opposed to the universal humanity idea) in the world of the pragmatical-successful personalities who are capable of fitting themselves into the impersonal technological world - as this was already pointed out in 1964 by W.C. Hallenbeck (HALLENBECK, 1964) - personalities who seem to successfully find in the world of electronics and cybernetics the answer to the challenges of modern living. Or, to put it in a different way using Toffler's words, it is a personality which has developed to perfection its adaptation OR-mechanism as it transformed itself also into a peculiar "technological system". For such as personality the biblical metaphorics are fully foreign while the basic or logo language is its intimate milieu. I have juxtaposed these two polarities - the biblical metaphoric and the cybernetic symbolic - because I am of the opinion that they illustrate pointedly the current situation of the human spirit as we are nearing the 1990s, and through this the actuality of the nature of adult education, especially in higher education.

For adult education I see a way out of this paradox situation in a stronger orientation towards the nature of man, towards the idea of "to be", an orientation towards eternal human and educational values or the pedagogy of essence as it is stressed by Dr. Bogdan Suchodolski (SUCHODOLSKI, 1974). Such orientation is in my conviction a justified reaction to the pragmatic direction of the current education of youth, to its proverbial insufficiency with respect to continuing cultural and spiritual values and to humanism. I am positive that the 1990s will make this idea very actual in higher adult education. At the same time this is the reason for a greater expansion of the depth of the theory of adult education, and especially in the nature of this activity, because adult educators are becoming more and more the subject of the politics of education. Should we succeed in this, we will have considerable influence in adult education, and especially in higher education, and this is something we all are much concerned about.

Continuing education for adult educators
Given the increasingly rapid accumulation of knowledge, also in andragogy, and thus the possible rapid dequalification of professional adult educators, continuing education for qualified adult educators will assume more and more practical significance. In my considered opinion it is unavoidable to develop a special higher education system for the continuing education of adult educators, based on validated models throughout the world. What are these models?

Training Systems

Based on empirical studies carried out in Yugoslavia, which summarize views and opinions of adult educators (SAMOLOVČEV, 1979b) I have arrived at the following preferred structure of continuing education for adult educators :

1. peripatetic residential subject seminars;
2. weekend seminars on timely themes based on dynamic work style;
3. consultative meetings with outstanding specialists, based on previous guided independent study and held in various places ;
4. summer and winter schools which include seminars, panels, national and international discussions, tutorials, discussions, symposia, etc. (as have been organized in Yugoslavia for the last 30 years);
5. guided independent study based on correspondence and mass media, such as exists in theory and practice in the Federal Republic of Germany in the "centres for independent study" (VOLKER, 1979), and
6. workshops (often interdisciplinary) led by well known specialists, theoreticians and practitioners, utilizing markedly dynamic work style.

I would like to add two further very attractive forms of continuing education, which have been proven in practice, to the above list of preferred forms :

1. distance education of the Open Univerity type, and
2. computerized individual information system which promises increasing and widening possibilities, but which still at this stage lies outside the sphere of adult education.

The practice of higher education around the world, especially in countries with long tradition of adult education, offers a wealth of new inspirations and pointers also in the continuing education for adult educators.

Adult education research
Andragogy keeps developing its research work in harmony with university tradition and current orientation. This research activity reflects its twofold

problematic research orientation and institutionalization :

1. pure and applied research as integral component of university teaching and;
2. research aimed at the development of andragogy as a scientific discipline.

The research work which is part of the teaching process is important in the training of adult educators, irrespective of the level of the program. This research is diverse. Thus for example studies at the undergraduate level are primarily empirical (applied research), and descriptive historical and theoretical, while the research carried out at the master's and doctoral levels is concerned with discovering new knowledge and thus contributes to the scientific enrichment of andragogy, although the demands of graduate study and the particular science in which they are grounded remain a primary determinant. In this research activity at the undergraduate and master's levels, individual and group work are closely related (Universities of Nijmegen, Zagreb, Belgrade, Free University of Berlin) ; this contributes to the advance not only of the studies but also of andragogy as a science.

Research work aimed at the development of andragogy as a scientific discipline is carried out primarily in institutes for pedagogical and andragogical research, such as the Pädagogische Arbeitsstelle des DVV in Frankfurt/Main, Institut für Erwachsenenbildung at the Free University of Berlin, Andragogical Centre in Zagreb, Institute for Adult Education in Leningrad, and many other organizations and associations for adult education at the regional and international level. This work contributes directly to the scientific development of andragogy as is evident from the activities of the Pädagogische Arbeitsstelle in Frankfurt, the National Institute for Adult Continuing Education in the U.K., and the European Centre for Leisure and Education in Prague.

Lately, institutional research activities and university teaching in adult education have come to increasingly form a unity, which is something I consider as a positive development. This also forms a basis of a development of a broader mutual exchange of scientific information and research results. The International Council for Adult Education and the European Centre for Leisure and Education are leaders in this respect.

However, in spite of the widening spectrum of the research problems there are certain questions which, although they are extraordinarily timely, remain unresearched. I will give some examples which lend themselves to comparative study :

1. the orientation of the modern man and its educational implications;
2. intercultural communication and mutual cultural enrichment;
3. participation in adult education in context of didactical technique preferences, and
4. information models in adult education.

The thematic possibilities of research quite obviously are much broader. The singled out topics can be found within the total spectrum, which through its timeliness can also spur on comparative studies which are more and more the way of the future for adult education as a science.

Summary
      The existence of many training programs for adult educators, which are conceptually diverse not only on a world scale but also at the national level demonstrate a relatively developed theory and practice of adult education. In spite of the evident stagnant occurrences and crises in adult education worldwide, especially in the 1980s, the training of adult educators in non-degree and in degree programs is becoming more and more of a new worldwide movement which in my opinion will also lead to new models of training. Several countries (Asia : Japan, China, South Korea and Thailand; South America : Venezuela and Brazil; and Africa : Tanzania and Zambia) already illustrate this development.
      I believe that this gathering at the Catholic University of Leuven also will bring a valuable contribution in this respect.

REFERENCES

Gieschler, S. et al. (1977) 'Anmerkungen von jenen, die auszogen, das Projektstudieren zu lernen - Auswertung von zwei deutsch-niederländischen Seminaren', Erwachsenenbildung, 17
Hallenback, W.C. (1964) 'The Role of Adult Education in Society', Adult Education, Outlines of an Emerging Field of University Study, Adult Edu-

cation Association of the U.S.A.
Knoll, J.H. (1973) <u>Einführung in die Erwachsenenbildung</u>, Walter de Gruyter, Berlin-New York
Kujundžić, N. (1979) 'Struktura/lik/suvremenog odgajatelja', <u>Savremene koncepcije i perspektive obrazovanja nastavnika</u>, Pedagoški zavod Vojvodine, Novi Sad
Olbrich, J. (1977) 'Erwachsenenpädagogik an der Freien Universität Berlin', <u>Erwachsenenbildung, 17</u>
Radlińska, H. (1947) <u>Oświata doroslych</u>, Ludowy institut oswiaty i kultury, Warszawa
Samolovčev, B. (1963) <u>Obrazovanje odraslih u proslōsti u danas</u>, Znanje, Zagreb
Samolovčev, B. (1979) <u>Opšta andragogija</u>, IRO Veselin Maslesa, Sarajevo
Samolovčev, B. (1979b) <u>Osposobljavanje andragoskih kadrova u SAP Vojvodini</u>, Andragoško društvo i Zajednica NU i RU Vojvodine, Novi Sad
Smith, R.M., Aker, G.F. and Kidd, J.R. (eds) (1970) <u>Handbook of Adult Education</u>, The Macmillan Company & A.E.A. of the U.S.A., London, New York, Toronto
Šoljan, N.N. (ed.) (1985) <u>Adult Education in Yugoslav Society</u>, Andragoški centar, Zagreb
Suchodolski, B. (1974) <u>Tri pedagogije</u>, Duga, Beograd
Turos, L. (1975) <u>Andragogika</u>, PWN, Warszawa
Volker, O. et al. (1979) <u>Offenes Weiterlernen, Erwachsenenbildung im Selbstlernzentrum</u>, Westermann Verlag, Braunschweig
Wroczyński, R. (1966) <u>Wprowadzenie do pedagogiki spolecznej</u>, PWN, Warszawa

Chapter Fourteen
ADULT EDUCATION AND THE COMPUTER

Thomas P. KEENAN
The University of Calgary
Alberta, Canada

Abstract
Computers will play an increasingly important role in adult education in the 1990s. Today's high school students will be a primary adult education 'market' then. They will be totally at ease with computer hardware and software, and will expect computer technology to be a part of their learning experience Older adults will also have increasing familiarity with computer technology. This paper reports on six years of experience in introducing computers into the young adult and adult education program at the University of Calgary.

Some of the most interesting possibilities involve using computers as knowledge archives and organizers. On-line databases and scholar's workstations provide fresh, new media for learning. In addition, computers are becoming a 'first-line' communications tool for many people. This capability opens up opportunities for adult education through data communication. It also creates some challenging cost and logistics problems. The latest developments in computer technology, such as artificial intelligence, raise hopes, which may be justified, for an adult education facility that is effective, pleasant, affordable, and most of all, humanized.

Introduction
The use of the computer in adult education is about to undergo a profound change. Fuelled by significant advances in computer and communications equipment, this development will have far-reaching implications for adult education in the 1990s.

Many of today's youngsters have computer knowledge and sophistication that would have characterized a graduate student a mere ten years ago.

Adult Education and the Computer

Consider these facts :

1. Students as young as eight years old have successfully completed coures in the Kids' Computer Camp we run at the University of Calgary. In the 1986 session their main assignment was to carry out analyses of telemetry data from the LANDSAT satellite.
2. Slightly older students are engaged in an international data communications exchange under the auspices of the Calgary School board. Just as their parents might have used scratchy 'ham radio', these students are using electronic mail with ease.
3. Gifted teenagers in the 'Shad Valley Program' have designed a sophisticated new computer modem; built extensive industrial software; and designed an experiment that was flown on the U.S. space shuttle.

The message is clear. As these students become the clients of the adult education system, we had better be ready for them ! They will expect computers as a natural part of the learning experience. And they will use them with skill and flair. Adult educators have the opportunity to capitalize on this enthusiasm, but could equally well 'miss the boat' on using computers effectively.

Computers and learning styles
Before discussing specific ways in which computers can enhance learning, let's look at some of the characteristics of computers that make them rather special :

1. Computers are 'mechanical'
This is true by the nature of computers, although some proponents of artificial intelligence might argue that their software shows non-mechanistic, almost human behavior. (Anyone who has ever stayed up all night trying to 'debug' a computer program knows that it can have a mind of its own!) In any case, being mechanistic is not all bad. Designers of computer assisted learning (CAL) materials cite this as an advantage. They point out that their programs are patient, tireless, and slow to anger at even the dullest student. Of course, experience

has shown that CAL students <u>are</u> quick to anger at dull programs !

2. <u>Computing knows no borders</u>
This means that information can be transferred, subject only to tariff and language barriers. Electronic transmission is as easy as a phone call, and has become a major means of acquiring 'public domain' software. Since running new programs is certainly an educational experience, many people are learning a great deal on their own in this fashion.

3. <u>Computers can put the learner 'in control'</u>
The feeling of 'being in control' of one's learning is particularly important to Adult learners. Malcolm Knowles makes this point in <u>Andragogy in Action</u> (KNOWLES, 1984). He suggests 'learning contracts' as a way to build commitment on the part of the adult learner. The use of computer techniques such as electronic mail, database searching, and computer conferencing, clearly puts much of the control in the hands of the learner. As a further example, Deidre Dale, writing in the <u>New Zealand Journal of Adult Education</u> (DALE, 1985) suggests that the elderly be taught the use of computer word processing programs. They could then use the program to "write memoirs, or recount incidents of personal or historical significance from their pasts". This shows a perceptive recognition of the fact that learners often have their own 'hidden agenda' in taking a course.

4. <u>Computers are fundamentally optimistic and future-oriented</u>
Since computers are a relatively new phenomenon, the majority of people with computer expertise are in the 25-40 year old age range. This is the age referred to by Bernard Lovell as a time when "most individuals have plenty of energy for all their interests and responsibilities... and much is likely to be achieved" (LOVELL, 1980). Computer people are used to fast change. Last year's 'hot' computer become's this year's 'doorstop' or 'boat anchor'. The assumption that computer equipment will get better and better has, to some extent, forced those working with computers to make their work

better to keep up with technology.

Let's turn now to some of the roles the computer can play in Adult Education, with an eye towards their potential in the near future.

Computers for computation
This is, of course the traditional role of computers. For years students have been 'running programs' to solve problems in mathematics and the natural sciences. However, there are some exciting new twists on this use of computers :

1. Students in the 'Shad Valley' program for gifted teenagers used an Apple IIe microcomputer to recreate the classical experiments in physics. So while Sir Isaac Newton had only his pulse as a timer, these students used the microsecond clock of the computer. In addition to learning about 'Newton's Laws' they were exposed to machine-language computer program. And they found the experience far more interesting than a traditional physics laboratory.
2. Many textbooks now come with a floppy disk attached. Students in courses from accounting to zoology can study concepts 'interactively' on a personal computer. This provides an additional instructional resource, outside of regular class hours. It may not make homework fun, but it seems to make it more interesting!
3. Supercomputers (e.g. the Cyber 205 which we have at the University of Calgary), have the power to allow even students to try computations that would have been impossible for anyone five years ago. This machine does 400,000,000 calculations per second. That is reckoned to be the equivalent of calculating 10,000,000 income tax returns per second !

Computers as a tool for communications
Personally, I feel this will be one of the most exciting areas of computer use in adult education. The basic mechanism is simple... computers are connected to (ordinary or special) telephone lines and people send messages between them. The simple pas-

sing of messages is referred to as 'electronic mail' (EM). If the parties are both on the system simultaneously, the word 'interactive' is often added.

A further development is the 'Computer conferencing system' (CCS) in which many people can enter their comments on a particular subject. The first time your use a CCS, it is like stumbling into a previously unknown treasure-house of interesting conversations. Most users are somewhat overwhelmed, but spend hours browsing through the system. They then fall into a 'steady state' where they check in periodically and reply to conversations of interest. I belong to about a dozen of these systems, and check into at least two or three of them every day. In fact, Professor Jacob Palme (PALME, 1985) has noted that he feels strangely "sad and cut off from the world" when he is unable to access his CCS.

Here are a few specific applications of this technology to adult education :

1. The University of South Florida CONGRESS project, described by Peter J. Dirr (DIRR, 1986) attempted to overcome what was called 'the loneliness of the long-distance learner' through the use of electronic mail. Students enrolled in a television course used electronic mail to obtain additional, out-of-class hours help.
2. Students from the 1984, 1985, and 1986 Calgary Shad Valley programs are able to stay in touch (for a very nominal fee) via the University of Calgary electronic mail system. As described in a separate paper (KEENAN, 1985) this has resulted in electronic learning of subjects as esoteric as the LISP programming language. (In fact, the LISP inquiry came from a student in British Columbia and was answered within hours by a computer expert in Paris, France.)
   The latest developments in the Shad Valley project include :
   - extensive discussion of joint projects that the students wish to start;
   - serious technical evaluations of computer equipment;
   - a fascinating series of discussions on Canadian university life (the students attend the program toward the end of their high school years, so most are now enrolled in University);

- a project aimed at building another electronic mail system.

Indeed observers of the Shad Valley program (which has existed since 1981) generally agree that the addition of the electronic mail component has been one of the most successful innovations in recent years (LANE-SMITH, 1986) :

1. The COSY system at the University of Guelph is an extremely successful, Canada-wide (actually international) forum for discussions, many of them about adult education issues.
2. No-one knows how much education goes on the public-access computer systems like The Source and Compuserve. These are commercial facilities that can be used, on a free-for-service basis, by anyone with a terminal or microcomputer. However, the following is certainly true :
   - at least one couple met, courted, and arranged to get married after meeting on this electronic medium;
   - several computer hardware and software vendors use these services to answer questions and provide customer support.

Another form of computer communication worth mentioning is the ability of computers to send 'videotex' images. Work in this field has been carried out in several countries, notably the Telidon project in Canada and the British Prestel and French Antiope systems. While North American videotex systems seem to be having a hard time, good progress has been made in Europe. The French Postal, Telephone and Telegraph agency has replaced its telephone book with computer terminals for 700,000 subscribers. As reported in Computerworld (GALLANT, 1985) "the French have made a national commitment to apply computer technology to everyday life". And they are reaping the benefits.

For several years, we have used Telidon videotex to supplement distance delivery courses at the University of Calgary (ELLIS, et al., 1983). While the instructor carries on a voice conversation with students at remote locations, both students and teacher look at an image displayed on a computer terminal. This provides a much needed visual component for teleconference instruction. Commercial 'electronic blackboards' are also available that do this job.

Computer-assisted learning
With all due respect to the many people who have worked on computer assisted learning programs over the years, it has certainly not lived up to its potential. Many education faculties have dusty boxes on the 1960s 'teaching machines' stored away somewhere. Those mechanical wonders gave way to electronic ones, but our understanding of how to use technology to teach has certainly lagged behind. There have been some noble attempts. The PLATO system, developed at the University of Illinois and now administered by Control Data Corporation, is certainly effective at teaching many subjects. There are several thousand courses available for the system. But the investment of millions of dollars that has been made in PLATO over the years is not paying great dividends.

For a while we could fault the technology. Computer assisted learning on small computers tended to be absurdly simple because of hardware limitations. Mainframe-based systems like PLATO required expensive computers and specialized terminals. Now the technology has caught up with our needs. A version of PLATO runs on a standard IBM PC microcomputer. What we are facing now are more basic problems concerning whether or not people want to learn from a computer, and if so, how they do it best.

Alfred Bork, in his book, Personal Computers for Education (BORK, 1985), describes some of the more promising developments in computer assisted learning. A closely related field is computer-managed learning (CML), in which the computer presents material and tests the students, but doesn't really try to 'teach'. There was an interesting application of CML in the province of Alberta recently. New regulations required that all ambulance drivers learn extra material and pass a recertification exam. Since they live in towns and cities all over the province, bringing them together was deemed infeasible. So instead, the Southern Alberta Institute of Technology organized a computer-managed learning system that allowed them to study the material at their convenience prior to writing the examination. It was, by all reports, well accepted. I believe this shows that people can learn by CML, but the problem of making them want to use this mode of learning is still unsolved.

Computer simulation and gaming

Computer simulation is a very powerful technique used in the design of everything from bridges to jet aircraft. It can allow the learner to ask 'what if' questions with impunity. Indeed, some of the disks that are being issued with textbooks allow students to manipulate the data to see what the effects would be. Gaming has similar objectives except that the opponent is usually a live human being. A game called PISCES was developed by Dr. Douglas Norrie and colleagues at the University of Calgary to simulate the world economy. The student is allowed to make social policy decisions and then, as the simulated time passes, see the effects. Outcomes range from prosperity to famine and pestilence, depending on the input parameters and certain random events.

In all games of this nature, the author is trying to make some point. No game, no matter how complex, could simulate the complexity of nature, so choices must be made. To the extent that these choices are sound, and the game 'feels real' they can be a valuable tool.

The Intercollegiate Business Game Competition (based at Emory University, Atlanta, Georgia, U.S.A.) relies heavily on computer simulation to test students' mettle in areas of planning and finance. They then have to make oral presentations of their results. Combining computer simulation with 'humanized' presentations seems to be an effective way of getting well-rounded performance out of the students. It could well serve as a model for future adult education use of these tools. The element of competition, used properly, also provides enough spice to keep the students excited about the business game competitions.

Computers as scholars' workstations

As more and more adult learners seek self-directed learning experiences, they will undoubtedly stumble into the area I call "the scholar's workstation". I have one in my office. With it I can :

   1. perform all the usual computer functions of word processing, spreadsheets, computation, etc.;

2. access the university's library catalog and find out what books we have on any subject;
3. find out if a given book is signed out or is (supposedly!) on the library's shelves;
4. search databases at the speed of light to find interesting/important things to read. This costs $10 - $100 an hour but you can accomplish a great deal in a few minutes though on-line searches;
5. correspond electronically with colleagues at universities around the world.

But I'm still not happy! To do the above requires <u>three</u> separate computers and my desk has long since overflowed. Anyway, I need the desk to hold the <u>manuals</u> for all those computers. In the future, we should be able to have a single, integrated unit that does all of the above and also :

1. contains a laserdisk with the most important reference works in your field (e.g. for medicine, the <u>Merck Manual</u> is already available on-line in a Canadian service called Infohealth/Infosanté);
2. accepts voice dictation and other commands;
3. perhaps even has an electronic 'sparring partner' to criticize new ideas;
4. is inexpensive enough for anyone to afford.

These objectives are not unattainable. All but the last two are possible today. Hopefully by the end of the century we'll see all this and even more features we can't even imagine hence don't know we need !

Computers as the window on tomorrow
What do we get when we put it all together? Some people fear a cold, dehumanized world of robot-like people 'interfacing' with faceless machines. I think they're wrong, or at least their scenario is unlikely. People like people. When we plan our courses we always make some provision for the social side of human beings. It may involve working together in teams, or sharing rides, or something as simple as a coffee break. But we always try to have that human contact around. Adult learners, by and large, are <u>learners by choice</u>. At our university, they are either paying their own hard-earned dollars, or convincing their employers to send them to

continuing education courses. All the computer technology in the world will not make them learn if they are unhappy while doing it.

In <u>Mindstorms</u> Seymour Papert argues that what an individual can learn and how it is learned depends on what models and materials are available (PAPERT, 1980). We've done pretty well with chalk and blackboards; you and I are products of that technology. But we're asking a great deal more from the next generation. They will be expected to vote intelligently in a society that faces questions like 'Star Wars' and 'Nuclear Power' and 'How to Control Terrorism'. You don't learn values on subjects like that from computers. However, many of these techniques, from international electronic messaging to computer simulation can give students the factual and conceptual backup needed to deal with an increasingly complex world.

REFERENCES

Bork, A. (1985) <u>Personal computers for education</u>, Harper and Row

Dale, D. (1985) 'Introducing elderly people to using computers', <u>New Zealand Journal of Adult Learning</u>, vol. 17, n°1

Dirr, P.J. (1986) 'Changing higher education through telecommunications' (presentation at World Congress on Education and Technology), B.C., Vancouver

Ellis, G.B. and Keenan, T.P. (1983) 'Microcomputers, videotex, and educational teleconferencing' in C. Keren and L. Perlmutter (eds), <u>Proceedings of the application of mini- and micro-computers in information, documentation and libraries</u>, Elsevier Science Publishers

Gallant, J. (1985) 'French apply high technology to their everyday lives', <u>Computerworld</u>

Keenan, T.P. (1985) 'Electronic learning : perspectives on maintaining an educational relationship through electronic communication' (International council on education for teaching), B.C., Vancouver (also available from ERIC)

Knowles, M. (1984) <u>Andragogy in action</u>, Jossey-Bass

Lane-Smith, D. (1986) <u>Personal communication</u>, Centre for creative technology, Canada

Lovell, R.B. (1980) <u>Adult learning</u>, Croom Helm Ltd., London

Palme, J. (1985) 'Computer conferencing is more than electronic mail', <u>Proceedings : computer con-</u>

ferencing and electronic messaging, Guelph, Ontario, Canada, 3-10

Papert, S. (1980) Mindstorms : children, computers, and powerful ideas, Basic Books

For Product Safety Concerns and Information please contact our EU
representative GPSR@taylorandfrancis.com
Taylor & Francis Verlag GmbH, Kaufingerstraße 24, 80331 München, Germany

www.ingramcontent.com/pod-product-compliance
Lightning Source LLC
Chambersburg PA
CBHW060603230426
43670CB00011B/1952